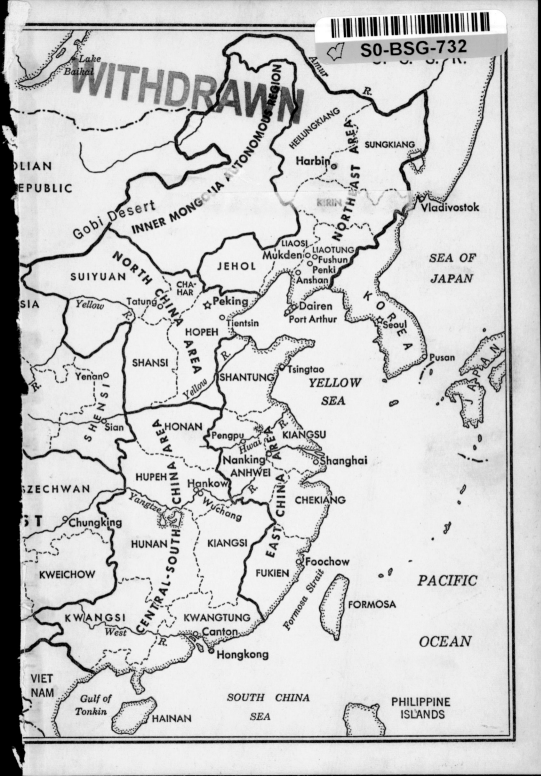

REPORT ON
MAO'S CHINA

951.05
M79r

30830

THE MACMILLAN COMPANY
NEW YORK · CHICAGO
DALLAS · ATLANTA · SAN FRANCISCO

THE MACMILLAN COMPANY
OF CANADA, LIMITED
TORONTO

REPORT ON MAO'S CHINA

FRANK MORAES

New York, 1953

THE MACMILLAN COMPANY

To the Memory
of
My Father
Most Selfless of Men

INTRODUCTION

This book is the fruit of a tour of Communist China which I visited in April–June, 1952, as a member of the Government of India's cultural delegation. It was my second trip to China. In 1944–1945 I was in Chungking and Kunming as a war correspondent. To some extent these two visits have enabled me to make a comparative study of China in the last days of Chiang and in the first years of Mao. The views I express are necessarily personal and my own.

My thanks are due to my colleagues, Donald Thomas and Mahendra Desai, who were kind enough to read parts of the manuscript and give me the benefit of their comment and friendly criticism.

F. M.

Bombay, India

CONTENTS

1. DELHI TO CANTON 1
2. MADE IN MOSCOW 13
3. CATCH 'EM YOUNG 25
4. "THE LAND IS OURS" 42
5. RULERS OF CHINA 59
6. HAMMER AND SICKLE 77
7. DOWN THE HWAI RIVER 91
8. MÄDCHEN IN UNIFORM 101
9. WHAT PRICE CULTURE? 114
10. ECONOMICS OF LIVING 126
11. AS MAO DECREES 146
12. SHANGHAI BLUES 159
13. FIVE STARS 172
14. GANDHI, NEHRU, AND MAO 187
15. INDIA AND CHINA 204

1

DELHI TO CANTON

Canton was another half-hour's flight. Hainan was a speck in the sea. Below us sprawled the monster earth of China.

From the air the jade-green, terraced paddy fields made an arresting pattern. Small clusters of villages speckled the countryside. Here and there the arched black roofs of houses rose like daubs on the landscape.

I was back in China after eight years. Memory recalled my last visit in the winter of 1944, when as a war correspondent I had flown over the Hump from an airfield in the northeast corner of India to Kunming. The Japanese were at that time thrusting towards the American bases in Hunan and Kwangsi. We had taken off from our Indian airfield two hours after midnight and flew high through grey vapoury clouds in an inky void. Coming at dawn over the plateau of Yunnan I saw the lights of Kunming.

The cold was numbing. It oozed through the thick soles of my United States army boots and through my fur-lined gloves. Sitting inside that huge lumbering plane in huddled heaps wrapped in greatcoats and rugs, with parachutes strapped to our backs and oxygen masks on our faces, we looked like phantoms from a Wellsian nightmare. "You don't have to be crazy to fly over the Hump," they said. "But, gee, it helps!"

I was going now in a different and more impressive capacity as a member of the Government of India's cultural delegation to China. We were fourteen, and heading the delegation was Mrs. Vijayalakshmi Pandit, sister of our Prime Minister. Mrs. Pandit, former Ambassador to Moscow and Washington, is decorative and petite. The shampooed sleekness of her white coiffure would distract attention from the burnished gold of many blondes.

"She should make up for our cultural deficiencies," murmured a journalist colleague, Chalapathi Rau, who edits the *National Herald* at Lucknow.

We flew to Mao's China in a Skymaster, and the fact that it was chartered from one of India's leading capitalist concerns, the House of Birla, seemed oddly amusing. "Fly the Birla way" ran the legend on the landing ramp. The lively amiable air hostess whose blue uniform blended with the plane's blue décor flitted up and down the gangway. Her friendly smile was also professional.

"It reminds me," said Raja, "of Tennyson's idea of freedom."

"Why?"

"It keeps broadening from passenger to passenger."

Raja Hutheesing, who is Nehru's brother-in-law, was not a member of our delegation; but he accompanied it throughout China as a representative of an Indian news agency. Opposite us sat the artist, Bendre, and the dancer, Shanta Rau.

Bendre, awake while others slept, had not been idle. He was working furiously on some sketches, and when I awoke he confronted me with a wide grin and a pencil sketch of myself lost in somnolent rapture. Shanta was to be a great success as a dancer in China, but the air was not her métier. She felt queasy and looked it. The sparkle had gone from her dark, darting kohl-fringed eyes, and her tapering hands were twisted in mudras of despair.

We had left Delhi the day before, stopping en route at Bangkok for the night. It had been my third visit to Siam's exotic capital.

The air of Thailand enervates. Its culture cloys with a "pretty-pretty" oppressiveness, but the Siamese, by nature more an island than a mainland people, are gracious and hospitable. Temperamentally they have many affinities with the Sinhalese. I enjoy watching their national dance, the *rum wong*. Its enchantment lingers like the fragrance of musk on muslin.

With Raja and an English friend and his wife we had made a round of Bangkok. It was our last glimpse of the capitalist world for six weeks.

* * *

Slowly our plane circled over Canton and dipped down to alight on the runway, in a bowl of green fields ringed by hills.

The flags fluttered. The bands brayed. Schoolgirls tripped forward to greet us with flowers. They were rosy and red-cheeked, and their eyes smiled beneath their mops of jet-black hair. Nearly every one of them wore the red scarf of a Young Pioneer. Behind them stood a thin long line of local dignitaries headed by Canton's Vice-Mayor. In their peaked caps and blue cotton uniforms, with buttoned-up jackets and trousers, they looked like a row of drab and slightly dingy marionettes. They bowed in friendly greeting and shook hands.

"Everything new originates in Canton," runs an old Chinese saying. But Canton itself was bedraggled. We drove in a long cavalcade of cars to the Guest House in the former foreign settlement which stands on a reclaimed sandbank known as *shameen* in the swarming Pearl River. A narrow canal separates the settlement from the city front. On the other side of the canal is one of the main thoroughfares, fringed by tall dishevelled buildings which face the bund. Plaster peeled from their façades, and they badly needed a coat of paint. Most buildings in the city had the same sad dispirited look.

"Canton has always been untidy," remarked an American acquaintance on my return from China.

But it wasn't that. Cities have a personality and individuality of their own. They express the ethos of their inhabitants and, in some ways, are strangely human. Bombay has changed since Prohibition. From a gay, generous, cosmopolitan city she has shrivelled into something frowzy and furtive. Like Rome, Peking has the air of a proud, remote, imperial being, untouched by the tempests around her. Nanking is ambivalent, a city of no loyalties nurturing the green loveliness of her environs and the meanness of her urban core. Shanghai is like a commercial colossus come to grief. She broods uncertainly, but defiance simmers beneath the surface. Canton exudes tragedy. Like a lost soul, she seems to be groping in a twilight dank with a sense of taint and terror.

So at least it seemed. The air of Canton oppressed me. There was something mildewed in the atmosphere despite the sunshine and the exhilaration which seizes one with new surroundings. It wasn't the meanness of the city's visage, for laughter walks in the dingiest of alleyways.

As we sauntered next morning down the bund, truckloads of workers drove past on their way to work. Some of them sang, their voices rising and falling shrilly to the waving arms of a cheer leader. Processions of children walked by. They marched in rows of four behind red fluttering flags to the clash of cymbals and the beat of gaily coloured drums. Off and on other, less lively processions moved by. There were workers clad in oily shining black with straw hats slung across their backs. They shouted slogans, and their raucous cries echoed harshly in the thin morning air.

"It's something out of this world," I remarked to Raja. "It's like visiting a new planet. But it doesn't hang together. There's a piece out of place. I wonder what it could be."

It teased me as we moved along. Around us were the patient plodding Chinese, much as I had seen them eight years before away across China at Chungking in the province of Szechwan. There were old men with lined, wrinkled faces which might have been carved out of ivory. The children, grubby and pudding-faced, seemed healthy. Pedlars plied their wares. Earnest, spectacled students walked swiftly by. Inside the shops, eyes peered at you from behind loaded counters.

You missed the elongated gowns of the men and the slit skirts of the women. Nearly every one of them now wore the new uniform garb of blue buttoned-up jacket and trousers. Transport had been more primitive in wartime Yunnan. On Kunming's cobbled streets, carts with rubber-tired wheels had swayed behind shaggy diminutive ponies which might have stepped straight out of a nursery print complete with tufted fetlocks and swishing tail. Often in Chungking I had stopped to watch officials and other persons borne high up the hillside in sedan chairs on the straining, sweating shoulders of grunting coolies.

Chungking was distant and different. But Canton was different too—different with a sameness which irked and irritated. It was as if a picture you knew well was inexplicably out of focus. All around, as we strolled down the bund, were bustle and activity. In China, unlike India, people seem always to be on the move. The Chinese seem to have taken to heart the biblical injunction to toil.

"I wish I knew what was wrong with the picture," I said to Raja.

Under the trees along the roadside were groups of workers and students clustered together in debate and study.

"Earlier this morning," remarked Raja, "I came across a sixteen-year-old boy indoctrinating some six or seven children. I asked him through Chang what he was doing. He was preaching against wastage."

Chang, our interpreter, was eager to explain most things.

"These," he said, pointing to an earnest-looking group, "are workers learning patriotic songs. And that student over there is teaching his group of workers how to read and write."

A board with a few ideographs stood up against a tree, and a student with the help of a stick was explaining the characters.

"Are the workers anxious to be literate?"

"Of course," said Chang. "Who wouldn't be?"

The workers did not get time off for this chore. It was part of their leisure routine. They sat in huddled groups around their instructors, much as any similar group of adult learners elsewhere. Some of them were animated and keen. Others watched listlessly through sleepy eyes.

Interspersed between these open-air classes and sitting separately were knots of students and other men. Some of the boys were barely out of their teens, but the tempo of their talk was lively. Watching them more closely, you detected a pattern. Each group operated under the tutelage of a single individual.

"Are these thought control classes?" I inquired tactlessly.

Chang looked pained. "Not thought control," he corrected. "Thought reform. Only Americans control thought."

"Do they? How?"

Chang hesitated for a moment. "The Committee on Un-American Activities," he said simply, and turned our attention elsewhere.

Chang, stolid and unemotional, was likable. His brown, bright eyes missed nothing. Although we tried him often his spirit never wilted. He was monumentally patient. He never thawed and he rarely relaxed. Only once, much later, did he speak of his fiancée and his impending marriage. He told us little of his boyhood apart from the fact that he came from "near Shanghai." We discovered by accident that he spoke French. He talked often, as the other interpreters did, of "peace and Asian friendship." And, like them all, his hatred of America was pathological.

The Guest House, wedged between the canal and the river, swarmed with mosquitoes. They made sleep impossible.

"You know, Chang," I remarked lightly one morning. "The mosquitoes kept me awake last night. They sucked my blood. From today I shall call them landlords."

"No," said Chang sombrely. "Call them American aggressors."

In Chang were centred the two focal points of Communist

dogma—loyalty to the State and hatred for those who differ from or oppose it. And of a sudden I saw the picture clear. Many years ago in Fascist Rome I had watched Mussolini's black-shirted youth swagger through the morning sunlight with drums beating and flags flying. Then as now the sense of something superimposed on a pattern old as time prevailed. Aeons of strife, culture, glory, and gore went into the making of these peoples whose strands reached back to Han and Hun, to Cicero and Confucius, to a many-splendoured past mirrored in the palaces and pageants of Peking and of Rome. And I thought: Now I know where the pattern is out of place.

Cathay, tired, wise, and ancient, lingered in many thoughtful eyes. But another China was astir, and the bustle of its coming was like the ripple on some luminous lake when a stone has shattered its calm. New lights shimmered on the surface, quivered and danced, and the waters shook convulsively, caught between pain and joy.

Here is where the dissonance lay. It was harsh and horrid. It was the mating of bamboo with blood and iron.

We were only two days in Canton, but I think I saw China for the next six weeks through the eyes of this brooding city. Something of its melancholy seized me. It would always be the same in our journey through China as the pattern repeated itself in a cycle: children drilling in the sunlight; workers marching; songs; dance; the weaving, rhythmic *yang-ko;* students militant with a new mood and movement; the vast regimented pattern of a China awake and alive; blue uniforms; blood-red flags; the gleam of gold as the cymbals crashed.

And underneath? Some of the saddest eyes in Canton looked at you from behind shop counters. They were the eyes of petty merchants and small traders.

On our second morning in Canton, Raja and I saw a crowd milling around a grocery store whose entrance was gay with banners, streamers, and flags. Inside the store a man was speaking with what seemed even to our untutored ears to be the accents of denunciation. Other men murmured and gesticulated. Behind the counter at the far end a man sat silent with his head bowed.

"What's going on here?" asked Raja.

"A workers' meeting," said Chang hastily.

"In a grocery store?"

Chang stopped in his stride. His face was wry. "Wu Fan," he murmured.

Two cryptic words. But what a wealth of meaning they conveyed!

Wu Fan (literally, the Five Antis) was a movement which had been under way more than four months when we arrived in China. It was complementary to San Fan (the Three Antis), another movement from which in fact it derived. Both ended shortly after we left China, but throughout our stay we came across many of their manifestations.

Until these movements were started it had been axiomatic in Mao's China, "A Communist is not corrupt, and who is corrupt cannot be a Communist." But money has a lure for Marxists no less than for meaner men. San Fan was the answer to this fall from grace. It sought to root out corruption, waste, and bribery from the party and official ranks. A little later the offensive was extended against "the contaminators," or commercial classes. According to the Communist rulers, these were primarily responsible for corrupting their new official cadres, which are drawn largely from the rural areas and have proved peculiarly susceptible to the lure of urban pelf and power. Hence, Wu Fan.

We joined the crowd around the grocery store and peered in. Inside, the denunciation continued.

"What is he saying?"

"He is calling upon the shopkeeper to confess," said Chang.

"Confess what?"

"His sins. He is an evil man. He has hidden his profits from the workers."

"And are they asking him to disclose them?"

"Yes. And other sins."

"What if he doesn't?"

"He will be tried in the People's Court."

"And if he does?"

"Maybe they will let him off with a light punishment."

The shopkeeper sat behind his counter, and his head was bowed. He may, for all I know, have been as Chang said "an evil man"; but his crumpled face and weary eyes bespoke resignation and defeat. The fight had gone out of him. He seemed old, forlorn, lonely, and pathetic.

"Let's get out of here," I said to Raja.

Perhaps men stir to the smell of blood. The place had a fascination of its own, and that evening our footsteps turned towards it again. But the store was closed, and the pavement empty.

Canton filled my mind with its contradictions and conflicts. In the musty fastness of the Guest House I tried to resolve them.

What manner of movement was this that set men howling in packs at a lone being in their midst, that brought into personal and political relationships the feline feel of the jungle? And yet light moved amid the shadows. There was spring in the step of China's youth, and the bliss of a golden dawn in its eyes. Magic touched the masses as if a wizard's wand had waved over them, conjuring them into beings lit with a new impulse and resolve.

Of course the pattern was superimposed. Men were being regimented into robots. But between the government and the vast mass of the people was a sense of communion unknown and unfelt in the long twilight of Chiang's China. Why should it be so? Had democracy failed? What strange alchemy gave Communism in China this fervour and form?

My thoughts, troubled and confused, raced back to a wintry evening in Chungking eight years before, when Chiang Kai-shek had granted me a private interview. I had secured it by vast effort and effrontery.

"I've got to see the Generalissimo," I told the Information Minister, mild-mannered Dr. Wang Shih-chieh, adding quite unfairly, "I'm the only Indian war correspondent in Chungking."

Wang shrugged his slight shoulders and pointed helplessly at the names of the American and British correspondents on the waiting list.

Later, I lunched with Dr. T. V. Soong. He was polite but provocative. I liked his lively and inquisitive mind. He asked some searching questions, and I answered frankly. His answers were equally frank, but he was careful to point out that they were "off the record."

"If there's anything I can do for you," he said in an unguarded moment, "please let me know."

"I want an interview with the Generalissimo."

His face fell. "It's difficult, but I shall try."

Three days later I got the interview.

I was asked to submit my questions a day before the meeting, and in the anteroom when the time came Hollington Tong, who acted as the interpreter, begged me not to go beyond them. "Holly" was nervous. I promised. Throughout the interview he sat perched on the edge of his chair, and though it was cold the sweat glistened clammily on his forehead.

The awe which Chiang excites in his entourage must be considerable, I thought. To me the Generalissimo was friendly, even cordial. He wore a khaki uniform, and I was struck by the stillness of his carriage. Off and on he cleared his throat with an odd disconcerting, rasping grunt.

India's Congress leaders were then in jail. Chiang inquired about them. He never once mentioned Gandhi, but he asked solicitously after Nehru: How was he? Where was he imprisoned?

India and China. Nehru and Chiang. Nehru and Mao. How quickly the pattern had changed!

Ruthlessness was characteristic of both the man from Hunan

and the man from Chekiang. Both achieved dizzy eminence and one still stays poised on the heights. Canton was the scene of their early efforts, and it was from a Cantonese, Sun Yat-sen, that both had imbibed their political philosophy.

Chiang failed because he believed primarily and entirely in himself. He was China. In his cold, complex calculations he overlooked one small item. He forgot the Chinese people. He believed that he and he alone could lift them by their bootstraps to bigger things, and his habit of using men as pawns irrespective of their personal or political integrity paved the way in the end to his downfall. Chungking stank with the odour of corruption. Personally incorruptible, Chiang was careless of the corruption around him so long as those who served him remained the instruments of his will. Between his government and his people yawned a gap which grew wider with the years.

"The Japanese," he said in 1941, "are a disease of the skin. The Communists are a disease of the heart." He knew the malady, but the remedy eluded him. In the end even his diagnosis was proved wrong, for the Reds spread like a rash over China's ailing body and simultaneously ate into the vitals of the Kuomintang.

Mao, starting from different premises, had reached a different conclusion, and Canton, scene of the Communists' early reverses, was now the stage of their triumph. It was a different world from the Chungking I knew. It wasn't that democracy had failed, for Chiang's government was never a democracy but only an oligarchy of personal power. Sun Yat-sen's Three Principles stood. But the men who carried his banner had fallen by the wayside.

So I mused, faced with the spectacle of a new China, puzzling, tremendous, and strangely novel. We could not judge her by the norms of our own way of life, for here was a tempo of being which moved and pulsated to stimuli different from ours. And yet could the human personality so surrender its individual self as to merge its being in a mechanism where every cog had its patterned place and ordered purpose? Ideas are explosive things, and Chiang, who had power and the means of violence, lacked ideas. Force, he thought, was the answer to most problems. With Kipling's Baron he believed that "iron—Cold Iron—is master of them all."

China's new ruler wields force but he also has ideas. On the Communists' own admission more than two million Kuomintang "bandits and reactionaries" have been liquidated in the three years since Mao Tse-tung assumed power. Force in itself could never forge into being the furnace of activity which is Communist China. What other fuel stokes it? I think the answer lies in the methods by which the new regime has created in the public mind the feeling that in working for the national welfare each individual labours for his own good. By making it appear as if the people were associated with the government at all stages, including the judicial plane, the Communists have made them privy to the government's acts and decisions. Thereby they have achieved a dual purpose. They have identified the people with the government and, by doing so, have prevented public criticism of the regime.

In Canton I perceived the first faint outlines of this subtle and sinister process. The picture was to fill in as we moved along on our journey. But at Canton for the first time I recognised a technique which created individual pride in collective action, and I realised how the personality of a people could be beaten out of shape to fit the pattern of its rulers.

2

MADE IN MOSCOW

"The identification of the Chinese people with their government is the heart of the matter," said K. M. Panikkar, our Ambassador to Peking. "Once you understand this, you understand China."

We were talking on a May morning in a courtyard of the Indian Embassy shortly after our arrival in Peking. Sunlight flooded the tiled pavement, and through the haze of shrubbery the air seemed golden.

Panikkar sprawled in a cane chair. He wore his spade beard like a talisman. His eyes, behind his spectacles, were alert and wary. I have known him for many years, and speech with him is always stimulating. In his company conversation becomes an intellectual exercise.

"That depends on what you mean by 'the people,'" I countered.

"Exactly," said Panikkar. "By 'the people' the Chinese government means all but three classes. These are called the unfriendly classes."

"And they are?"

"Landlords, the antigovernment elements in the Kuomintang, and what are known as bureaucratic capitalists."

Most people have a conversational mannerism. Panikkar's consists in tilting his head until it snuggles almost on his shoulder in the manner of a spry cockatoo. He does this when emphasising or expounding a point.

"Bureaucratic capitalists," he explained, "are officials who've exploited their position to amass money—like X," he added with a gleam of malice, naming a well known public figure in India.

"These three classes," he continued, "are outside the civic pale. They have no rights, but the people have supralegal rights against them. For instance, no special legislation would be required to deprive Chiang Kai-shek or T. V. Soong of his properties in China."

Panikkar, I knew, was a not inconsiderable landowner in his native Malabar. Perhaps the same thought occurred to him.

"I've come to the conclusion," he sighed, "that the Chinese regard landownership as intrinsically antisocial. On the other hand, their attitude to private capital is not so rigid."

"Do they accept the capitalist?"

"Oh, yes! He's one of the recognised four friendly classes. Of course he's lowest in the scale. The proletariat, or industrial workers, come first; then the peasants; then the petty bourgeoisie, or small traders; and finally the national bourgeoisie, or capitalists."

Panikkar went on to speak of the realism of the Chinese Communists. They know, he explained, that increased production is a prime imperative. So they tolerate the capitalist because of his experience and know-how. And even in the agricultural field they maintain a system of fine gradations. The landlords are dispossessed; but in many areas the "rich" peasant is tolerated. All this, of course, is temporary. The Communist regime admits that China is only in the penultimate stage of the Socialism which Russia has achieved. Peking is a step behind Moscow.

"When China achieves her nirvana," he concluded, "peasant

ownership will be abolished, the land will be collectivised and the capitalist will be merged in a classless society."

Panikkar was echoing what I had heard before. At a banquet given in Canton by the Mayor, General Yeh Chien-ying, I had started a mild discussion on land reforms with the secretary-general of the local Municipal Executive. He was a thoughtful-looking man, and spoke with quiet emphasis. Peasant holdings, he conceded, were only a temporary feature of Communist China. Later the State would acquire the land; but the peasant would remain free to sell his produce as he did now, paying his dues to the State. The capitalist, again, was tolerated because his coopera-tion was necessary to industrialise the country; but he too would go. "Ours," concluded the secretary-general, "is a Chinese revolu-tion. Therefore it had to be different."

I retailed the conversation to Panikkar.

"If their revolution is Chinese," I remarked, "why is it that Mao's picture is always flanked by those of Marx, Engels, Lenin, and Stalin?"

These portraits invariably hang together in public halls, in-stitutions, and other centres throughout the country.

"But that's the Apostolic Succession," said Panikkar. "It proves nothing. If it had a Soviet connotation what are the two Germans, Marx and Engels, doing there? Besides they lived long before the Bolshevik Revolution. They had nothing to do with it. Marx, Engels, Lenin, Stalin, and Mao. You see? The Apostolic Succes-sion. Nothing more."

Panikkar was right in insisting that Marxism, not Bolshevism, was the leitmotiv of this picture parade. But his argument had one transparent flaw. If Marx and Engels had nothing to do with the Bolshevik Revolution, then Voltaire and Rousseau had no place in the French Revolution. Maoism stemmed from Marxism via Bolshevism, and in that sense it was derivative, not distinct. Its course was different, its methods varied, but the end was the same. The end was the Marxist State on the Soviet pattern.

The mistake of regarding the Chinese Communists as agrarian reformers sprang from the assumption that this intermediate stage represented the final phase. I remembered being puzzled by the same phenomenon in China eight years before, when I had posed this question to a Communist in Chungking. His reply was frank:

"We are not mechanical Marxists. Communism is conditioned by the circumstances of a country. It does not call for a prole- tarian dictatorship at every point. But it's nonsense to say that we are not Marxists."

In the discussion which had followed, the pattern of Maoist tactics and strategy had emerged more clearly:

China's Communists, explained my Red contact, believed in the methods enunciated by Marx and Lenin for solving their prob- lems. But Mao's men did not copy European methods wholesale. In China the conditions did not exist "for the pure, unadulterated practice of Communism." More than four-fifths of her people were peasants. Her industries were not developed. In the entire country there were only some three million industrial workers. And at that time Japan had invaded China.

"China's central problem," said the Communist, "is how to improve the livelihood of the peasants and lessen the exploitation of the landowners. What our peasants now demand is democracy. They are opposed to the landlords' oppression. They want free- dom of speech and organisation. The Japanese aggression in China is against all strata of the Chinese people. Our task is two- fold: to drive out the Japanese, and to improve the livelihood of our people. In achieving this the first thing is to organise a national revolution for the purpose of establishing democracy. Then we shall organise a social revolution in order to establish Com- munism."

Democracy? Communism? How were the two reconcilable? When the Communists spoke of securing democracy they meant the wresting of civil rights from the Kuomintang. It was proper that the peasants should have the right of free speech and organisation, as Mao demanded. But was Mao in turn prepared to extend similar concessions to his political opponents, or even to the peasants?

In the Marxist vocabulary "democracy" obviously means the right of the Communists alone to preach their dogmas and doctrines. The role of others is to hear and obey.

I remarked on this to Panikkar, observing also that the fount of inspiration was Russia.

He disagreed, insisting: "The Chinese revolution is Chinese. It has its roots in Chinese history. Only the Communist technique is imported from outside. That's foreign."

"You might say the same of Russia. Didn't the Allies in the First World War allow Lenin to pass from Switzerland to Russia in a sealed railway carriage like a microbe? The conditions in Russia were then equally ripe for revolution. But the fountainhead of Lenin's wisdom was Marx, not Moscow. That was foreign too."

Listening to Panikkar, I thought of the exuberant talent which had propelled him along so many brilliant and varied paths. It was a far cry from Patiala to Peking. At Patiala he had shone in the serpentine world of India's princely politics and served a maharaja as removed from democracy as chalk from cheese.

Panikkar's scholarship is prodigious. Backed by a massive memory he is able to draw analogies and cite precedents with the ease of a conjurer extracting rabbits from a hat.

"An authority on two closely associated subjects," commented an English judge dryly after watching his intellectual sleight of hand. "He knows his European ecclesiastical history and the Indian Princes."

Others were less kind.

"I make history," Panikkar once said in a mood of exaltation.

"You mean you make it up," said his companion.

Historians, it is said, put into the books they write the things from the books they read. Watching Panikkar, I could not help feeling that his sense of history had overwhelmed him. He saw himself projected into the drama of a great revolution, and its excitement had infected him.

"There's one difference between the Russian and Chinese revolutions," he went on. "The Soviet revolution was in a sense a *coup d'état*. Lenin and his followers had to experiment. They learned by a process of trial and error. But Mao's revolution was different. It was spread over twenty-odd years. The pattern was set in Yenan and other Red-ruled areas. And in the process the Communists reared their own armies and built up their own administrative cadres. That is one reason why the transition was effected so smoothly."

"But it wasn't so bloodless."

"Maybe not. Why?"

"I was thinking of the executions in 1950."

"Oh, those!" said Panikkar. "Never forget that Korea is the key to much that is happening in China. When Chiang fled to Formosa he left behind him large, scattered groups of Kuomintang guerrillas and antirevolutionaries. The Communists have an excellent intelligence set-up, and they were aware of their presence. But so long as there was no internal trouble or external threat they left them alone. When after the blow-up in Korea the American Seventh Fleet was interposed between Formosa and the Chinese mainland and there was talk of an invasion of China, Mao struck."

"Did the number of those executed run over two million?"

"Possibly, though I think the actual figure was less. But you've got to see these things comparatively. Only the other day I was reading an official French statement which gave the number of those liquidated in postwar France after the liberation as over ten thousand. Now, France has a population of only forty million. China's population is well over four hundred million."

Even so, I reflected, it would be a mere one hundred thousand against two million.

Panikkar talked of the Chinese character.

"Remember," he said, "that the Chinese are not revolted by

cruelty as we are. They would as soon slit a man's throat as they would a frog's. They would think no more about it. A prisoner in their reckoning is not entitled to humane treatment. He's man-acled hand and foot with a chain around his neck."

"Much as our own Moguls did."

"Exactly. You might think of the Manchus as the Chinese counterpart of the Moguls. The Moguls enjoyed flaying prisoners alive. The Manchus also ran to all sorts of refinements like slicing prisoners slowly to death. Notions of justice differ. You went to jail for seven years in Patiala if you killed a cow. Until ten years ago a Brahmin could not be hanged in Travancore."

Panikkar's nimble mind darted from topic to topic.

"What we've got to realise," he said, "is that a new power has emerged in Asia. When that happens the balance of power politics is upset. The Soviet revolution was the biggest fact which emerged from the First World War. We're too close to see clearly but it may be that Mao's China is the biggest fact to emerge from the Second World War."

Two days before, our delegation had watched the May Day parade in the great red square facing the Tien An Men, or Gate of Heavenly Peace. Here was the apotheosis of Communist China triumphant. Superb as a spectacle, it was also impressive as a demonstration of the emotion, fervour, and force which pieced and held together the massive mosaic of the new and militant China.

As the boom of guns reverberated through the square Mao took his place in the yellow-tiled pavilion immediately above our stand. He was in khaki uniform, and under the peaked cap his face was full and heavy. Off and on, he lifted his hand, palm upturned, in a flapping semi-Fascist salute. The rounded shoulders seemed out of place with the upright carriage.

Near Mao stood Chou En-lai, his figure silhouetted sharply against the sun. Chou, who is China's Foreign Minister, is one of the trinity around the Red leader. His two colleagues stood close by. General Chu Teh, a chunky figure with a roughhewn, wrinkled face, is chairman of the People's Revolutionary Military Council, a position virtually equivalent to that of commander-in-chief. Not far from him was the slim Liu Shao-chi, high priest of Red dialectics, whose countenance is wan. He wears the pallid look of a medieval monk. Liu, like Mao a Hunanese, is one of the six vice-chairmen of the Central People's Government and is Communist China's chief pamphleteer.

Alongside them were other notabilities of the regime. There was Peking's Mayor, Peng Chen, pugnacious of face but genial of manner, with whom I had had an interesting conversation some days before. At the extreme left stood the tall bearded Chang Lan, for all the world like a bedraggled prophet from the Old Testament. Chang is a non-Communist. He is chairman of the China Democratic League and a vice-chairman of the Central People's Government.

The square echoed to the tramp of Mao's legions. Resplendent in their scarlet scarves, the Young Pioneers led the march. They glowed with life. Cymbals chimed, drums rolled. Behind the vanguard of youth tramped the workers and peasants in their blue uniforms. White cloths swathed the heads of the peasant women. The petty bourgeoisie walked by, and after them the capitalists.

Now and again doves of peace were released and flew in grey, fluttering arcs over the square. The legions swung by, and rounding off the procession marched the national minorities—Tibetans, Thais, Koreans, Miaos, Mongolians, and Muslims. Their raiment was like Joseph's coat, of many colours, and as they walked their trailing, multi-hued garments made a rainbow splash. In the dappled sunlight gold mingled with red over a sea of blue.

It was a tremendous spectacle. For more than three hours some 500,000 men, women, and children had surged through the square shouting, singing, waving, and cheering in a tidal sea of exultant energy and exuberance.

I looked at the gold-lettered blood-red flags of the revolution high above their heads and wondered what impulse and ideas moved them. Was all this demonstration drilled and patterned? Surely some spontaneity seized them. It was political, but it was also primeval.

"The Chinese are a theatrical race," said a European diplomat to me the same day. "They love such shows. Chiang could have organised one though, of course, it would be nothing so spectacular. The Communists have learned the mechanics of such shows from the Russians."

If so, they have learned them well. By a dramatic simplification of the Chinese passion for histrionics the Communists have carried their politics to the people. The processes of public accusation, confession, and self-criticism which accompanied movements such as San Fan and Wu Fan would repel most foreigners, including Indians. But they are part of the Chinese pattern.

I raised the point now with Panikkar.

"Yes, there's a great deal to it," he agreed. "Thought control, for instance, is not foreign to the Chinese. For centuries they have been taught to restrict their reading to accepted and prescribed texts. What, after all, was Confucianism? A mixture of nature worship and ancestor worship. Of course it's no longer a State system. That was undermined as far back as 1911, when the republic was proclaimed; but it survives as a cult."

He might, I thought, be right. Had not Mencius, the interpreter of Confucius, held that goodness is developed by the study of the classics? To substitute the gospel according to Mao for the gospel according to Confucius conforms to this pattern. Confucianism does not derive from Confucius in the sense that he is the founder of the system. He is only the transmitter of the learning and lore of the ancients. In the same way Mao might embroider on the teachings of Marx.

By modelling the government upon the concept of a patriarchal family, Confucianism gave to the State the character of a large and close-knit family. By a similar process of thought trans-

ference the Communists have found it comparatively easy, while
subtly destroying loyalty to the family, to substitute for it loyalty
to the State.

The Father Image has long ruled Chinese thought and conduct.
The tradition of associating age with wisdom has deep roots in
the Orient, perhaps nowhere deeper than in China. Rarely does
the family question the decision of its head; and on the political
plane this attitude finds expression in obedience to the will of
the ruler.

Government in ancient China was based upon the supposed
relationship between Heaven and the Emperor. At the winter
solstice the Emperor in his role of high priest of the nation
worshipped Heaven. At the summer solstice he worshipped the
Earth. With the removal of the Emperor the people became the
rulers and looked to the Kuomintang to give them a new heaven
on earth.

For many years Chiang could exact the people's loyalty; and
only when he failed the people did the people fail him. Then the
Father Image became identified with Mao, and in the benignity of
his Buddha-like countenance China's millions saw the radiance of
new hope and life. Mao seemed to be the answer to their prayers.
To them he was a Messiah speaking a language they understood,
an idiom which was Chinese. If the people were the rulers, then
theirs was the earth and the glory.

Panem et circenses. Bread and circuses. How like a Roman
Emperor Mao seemed that day as, flanked by his Praetorian
Guard, he watched his legions tramping through the sunlit square
below!

The grip of the gentry had gone. But over China was a grip
stronger if less perceptible. It was not that the marching men,
women, and children resembled robots. A new alchemy had
changed the dross of their being into shimmering gold—or so it
seemed. In acquiring privilege they had lost power without knowing it. Perhaps power was intangible. But freedom, if they only
knew it, was as vital as food.

I said so to Panikkar.

"It's a question of priorities," he said. "Here in China freedom from want is a primary need. If you accept that you must accept the system of control which ensures it."

"Even to the point of thought control?"

"The Chinese are a practical people. They will give this regime their support until it proves itself unworthy. So far it meets their needs. It calls itself the People's Democracy, and in many ways it is that."

"I can understand," I said, "why formal democracy, as America and Britain understood it in the nineteenth century, is meaningless in backward countries like China and India. Governments have obviously a bigger role to play in our countries. In fact unrestrained liberty would mean anarchy, a license for everyone to run amuck. It would even destroy the ultimate prospect of our attaining true liberty."

"What's your objection then?"

"What I object to is the Chinese Communists' using democracy as a cloak or a means to achieve their end of Communism. They are using democracy to stifle democracy."

"Meaning?"

"So many people have been misled into thinking that Chinese Communism is something different. It isn't. It's different only in the fact that the so-called People's Democracy is a steppingstone, a springboard, to Communism. Only the Chinese call it Socialism."

"But they've never concealed it."

That, I reflected, was true. It was there in the speeches and writings of Mao Tse-tung as far back as 1940, and my own Communist contacts in Chungking had spoken of it in 1944. Why then did so many people romanticise the situation in China? Panikkar himself, on a brief return to India some months before, had described the Central People's Government as a coalition government of a democratic pattern.

It certainly included non-Communist groups. But it was not a representative government in the democratic sense as we understood "representative," for it arbitrarily excluded the "reactionary elements." Moreover the entry of the non-Communist groups into the Central People's Government committed them to the Common Programme, which in effect regarded this compromise as a temporary expedient. By coming in on those terms the non-Communists conceded that their own existence as separate co-operative units was ephemeral, and therefore signed their political death warrants.

The Chinese Communists saw democracy as a means, not an end. Away back in 1937 Mao had compared democracy to "rice which we get from Hankow—it takes time and costs money, and there are people who try to intercept it."

"Democracy," he then said, "is all the more difficult because it is intangible."

Now he was more specific. In a statement on July 1, 1949, the twenty-eighth anniversary of the founding of the Chinese Communist party, he referred to "the people's democratic dictatorship" and explained it:

"The right to vote is only given to the people and not to the reactionaries. These two aspects—namely, democracy among the people and dictatorship over the reactionaries—combine to form the people's democratic dictatorship."

Surely this was using democracy in order to stifle it. It was wielding the form to batter the spirit. Beneath the colourful crust of Communist China glowing with new life was a hard core of ruthless resolve and purpose. The trimmings of this Red cake were gay and pleasing. They made a pretty pattern. The ingredients were Chinese. But the recipe came from abroad. It came from Moscow.

3

CATCH 'EM YOUNG

She wore a red sweater, and her pigtails dangled tantalisingly over her shoulders. Sweet sixteen! Her English was fluent, and she spoke it with a marked American intonation.

It was Youth's Day, May 4. We were visiting Peking University. The young girl acted as interpreter to the president of the Students' Union, who was among those showing us around.

May 4 is an important day in modern China's calendar. On May 4, 1919, the students of Peking University had protested against their government's acquiescence in the Treaty of Versailles which awarded the former German concessions at Shantung to Japan. In the week-long demonstrations that followed, the students so whipped up public feeling that the government had found it impossible to sign the treaty.

For the first time China's intelligentsia realised that they could work hand in hand with artisans, shopkeepers, and workers. "The May Fourth Movement," in the words of Mao Tse-tung, "was an anti-imperialist as well as an antifeudal movement. . . . It was a Communist revolt without Communists." In June, 1921, the first Congress of the Communist party of China was held at Shanghai.

25

Now at Peking, in the vast auditorium where we were welcomed, speeches were made, and the students cheered tumultuously. From the dais, I looked upon rows and rows of young men and women reaching back to the far end of the hall. The place was packed. Students sat on the window sills, stood on ledges, overflowed into the aisles.

I found myself comparing the young people with their Indian counterparts. They seemed more disciplined and more lively. There was no jostling or shouting, no cries or catcalls. They gave an impression, individually and collectively, of keenness. In a theatre, they say, an American audience leans forward while a British audience leans back. These students conveyed a sense of leaning forward. I think Indian students are prone to lean back.

As we came out into the campus, teeming with life, the girl in the red sweater joined us. A company of Hungarians on a visit to Peking for May Day was teaching a group of Chinese students a Hungarian folk dance. They danced merrily and laughed often. Other groups of students were playing games, and the girls mingled freely with the boys.

The president of the Students' Union explained the significance of May 4. Thirty-three years ago the student demonstrators, after assembling opposite the Tien An Men, had visited the foreign legation quarters and called upon the American Minister. He had refused to see them. From the red-sweatered girl who interpreted as the president talked rolled a familiar chant of phrases—"American imperialists and aggressors," "the peace-loving, freedom-loving people of China."

Already we were inured to such forms of speech. But pouring like an incantation from the lips of this slender, lively slip of a girl, they made many of us feel self-conscious. Were they just routine phrases repeated mechanically? Or did they convey a special meaning to her? It was difficult to tell.

Only the day before, on a visit to Tsinghua University, also in Peking, I had come across a bright friendly student. I asked him whether his textbooks had been changed since "the liberation."

"Yes," he replied.

"Were they out of date?"

"No, they were the instruments of American cultural aggression."

He was an intelligent lad, perky and with a sense of fun. Until then he had spoken as any normal boy on a college campus. It was as if I had touched a button and released a robot reaction.

This was the idiom of Mao's China, and it was not confined to the young. At one of the many banquets given us in Peking I chanced to meet Peking's Mayor, Peng Chen, who is also a member of the Central Committee of the Communist party.

As it happened the only interpreter at hand was Paranjpye, an Indian attached to our Embassy, who speaks Mandarin fluently. I requisitioned his services.

Peng answered my questions but was restive. Within two or three minutes he had signalled across the room to a Chinese who came and sat with us. He was Peng's interpreter.

The conversation proceeded and concluded smoothly. Only once did the Chinese interpreter intervene to correct Paranjpye.

"The late Kuomintang Government," said Paranjpye translating an answer by Peng.

Quickly the Chinese interposed. "The reactionary regime of the bandit, Chiang Kai-shek," he corrected.

Communism has its own semantics in thought, word, and deed. In a Communist country language is as drilled as thought. It falls into definite patterns acquiring a distinct idiom which attaches equally to personalities and principles. Thus Chiang in Communist China's vocabulary will always be a "bandit" when he is not labelled a "Fascist." The Americans are "imperialists and aggressors." "Freedom-loving and peace-loving" are the natural attributes of the Chinese.

This was particularly noticeable at the children's nurseries we visited. Early during our stay in Peking we passed an afternoon at the Pei Hai Park and nursery. Much later, in the closing stages of our journey through China, we visited in Shanghai another children's nursery run by Madame Sun Yat-sen. She is the only woman among the six vice-chairmen of the Central People's Government.

Chinese children are irresistible. With their almond eyes, their mops of jet-black hair, and their porcelain faces they have the appearance of animated dolls. At both nurseries small concerts were staged, and the Korean war figured prominently on both programmes. Tiny tots marched in, carrying banners of Mao and Stalin. Some of them were dressed as guerrillas and waved red flags with the imprint of the hammer and sickle. They sang, as children do, in ragged chorus, stumbling over some of the words but quite obviously enjoying themselves. One item showed the child guerrillas shooting at an imaginary American plane.

At the Shanghai nursery the children ranged from two to seven years. It was not as impressive as the one in Peking, where the children seemed brighter and more cleanly dressed; but in a classroom we stumbled across an interesting item.

"These," said the woman director, pointing to some ideographs on a board, "are the Five Loves."

"The Five Loves?"

"Yes. Every child in China is taught the Five Loves: love for the fatherland, for the people, for labour, for science, and for public property." There was no mention of love for parents.

In the young mind the focus of loyalty is being shifted sharply from the family to the State. One of the prime objects of the ideological remoulding movement is to cut at the roots of filial obedience and domestic loyalties by transferring the old Chinese reverence for the head of the family to the head of the State. Like Confucius and Lao-tse but unlike Buddha, the Communists are concerned mostly with men and have no interest in God. The child is the charge not of its parents but of the State.

Youth has pride of place in the new China, and everywhere there was evidence of the government's concentration on the young. Peking's bookshops were stacked with Marxist literature and magazines. These were largely in Chinese, but a goodly proportion was in Russian. A few English books and magazines peeped from odd shelves. They included some British and American Communist journals.

A section of most bookshops was given to juvenile publications. Patterned on the Russian model, they were brightly produced and contained many coloured pictures. The Marxist motif predominated. Doves of peace flew alongside American soldiers fleeing before Chinese troops. Stalin smiled benignly from a page, and Mao strode across the landscape like a Colossus.

Almost every afternoon around four, hordes of school children descended on these shops and like devouring locusts cleared the counters of their juvenile load. Hardly one of them bought a book. They stood around scanning their booty, sat on benches and on the floor, each with a magazine or book clasped in his or her tiny hands, and all you saw was a bobbing of heads as they buried eager, inquisitive, incredulous noses in the pages. They read with the zest of American children reading their comics. The books were dutifully restored, and off and on a scamper of feet announced another arrival or departure.

China's Reds believe in "catching 'em young." With the workers and peasants, the children are the chief objects of indoctrination and demonstration. They form the main props in China's show window.

"The Chinese," said a British resident of some thirty years' standing, "will, of course, always be Chinese. They're individualists, but they're also amenable to discipline. They could be organised easily. If Mao's regime lasts another twenty years a generation will grow in China which thinks, talks, and does nothing but Communism."

That, of course, is precisely what the regime plans. Already the children seem to be exuberantly on the side of the government. Communism encourages the habit of doing things together. This has an instinctive appeal to the young. All the world over, children love to do—what other children do.

A theatrical streak runs in most Chinese, and this expresses itself in a liking for the colourful and spectacular. No youngsters react more strongly to flags, uniforms, drums, and cymbals.

"Did you watch how the children marched?" asked Leo Lamb, head of the British Negotiating Mission, on the evening of the May Day parade. "Like proud, prancing ponies."

So they did.

The nursery tots lisping songs of Stalin and Mao understood little of what they sang. But young minds are like sensitised photographic plates; and, exposed to the scene under the Communist sun, they would soon take on its image and pattern. In the process they would learn to know its meaning.

At times the very innocence of childhood triumphed over the indoctrination of age. A foreign diplomat at Peking told an interesting story. A Catholic nun who was head of an orphanage was arraigned for trial on a charge of cruelty to the young inmates. The older girls, duly indoctrinated and politically minded, supported the charge. But when the smaller children were produced as witnesses they stoutly denied it. They insisted in all innocence that they had been treated well. They had no complaints.

Among the first things the Communists did on capturing power was to organise the New Democratic Youth League, which is open to all Chinese under twenty-five. Although membership is voluntary, to belong to it is to be one of the juvenile elite. And since under a decree of the Central Committee of the Communist party membership in the League is compulsory for all young aspirants to party membership, the League card is a prized possession. Today the League counts some six million adherents, the number having grown nearly thirtyfold since early 1950, when the total on the rolls was approximately 200,000. It has about 250,000 branches throughout the country. Young peasants constitute more than 50 per cent of its membership, while youthful workers approximate 35 per cent. Students total some 12 per cent, and girls make up 30 per cent.

Though in a minority, the students form its intellectual core. Through them is propagated one of the chief aims of the League

—"to enrich the ideological contents of patriotic education on the basis of Marxism-Leninism and the Thoughts of Mao Tse-tung." The following oath is taken by student members at the inaugural ceremony: "I solemnly swear to follow the organisation, to follow its decisions, to follow the majority, to follow the people, to observe the organisation's rules and statutes, eternally to move forward with the Communist party, to study Mao Tse-tung's thought and cultural and scientific knowledge, and to apply every effort to self-reform so that I may be of service to labouring citizens."

Other chores, as they develop, are tacked on to these basic tasks. In 1951 members were required to take part in the Resist American Aggression and Aid Korea campaign. They are expected to support the land reforms and to help the government suppress the "counter-revolutionaries." Another patriotic duty is to enrol themselves for the military academies. Students are also called upon to display their loyal spirit by supporting the government's measures to take over the missionary schools.

As the elite corps of young China, members of the League spearhead all activities in schools and colleges. It is through them that the regime propagates its ideas and plans. Once the word comes from the top, the machine swings into action.

Alongside the League, which is primarily a youth organisation, are the Chinese Young Pioneers, who are teen-agers. They number over three million. Like members of the League the Young Pioneers are engaged in various kinds of extracurricular activities designed to promote and consolidate the Communist State. "Prepare yourselves," runs their slogan, "to struggle for the construction of the motherland and for the realisation of Chairman Mao's great ideal."

These movements constitute the germinating ground for the propagation of the Communist faith. As a teen-ager leaves his school for the university he moves from the Young Pioneers to the New Democratic Youth League, both of which are springboards for eventual membership of the Communist party. Education along with most other activities in China reflects a familiar technique—the application of the right pressure in the right direction at the right time. Indoctrination is a process extending literally from the cradle to the grave.

In a Communist State thought is a government monopoly; and in China today universities and schools are the natural vehicles for impressing Marxism on the young mind. All else is subordinate to that consideration. It looks as if Mao's regime is well on the way to winning young China to its doctrines. Youth, given pride of place in the new State, is also promised a new deal. Its aid is sought in building up a society where the old reverence for parents, scholars, and teachers will be replaced by a new reverence for the omnipotent State.

Inevitably the intellectuals, including the professors and the teachers, are equally the creatures of the State to whom their minds are mortgaged. How well the Communists have profited from Chiang's folly and mistakes! And how skilfully they have exploited these wavering individuals who for more than two decades stood poised precariously on the razor's edge which divides the indeterminate liberal from the determined Communist! The greatest threats to democracy are twofold—the unorganised majority and the organised minority.

In the final phases of Kuomintang rule, to be a liberal was to be suspect. A heavy toll was taken of academic centres of learning, and many professors and students died for their temerity in opposing Chiang's regime. During the closing years of Kuomintang rule the liberal elements cowered in the last ditch of the universities.

Their memories went back to Kunming in 1945 and earlier to Shanghai in February, 1931, when Jou Shih, disciple of Lu Hsun, now venerated as China's Gorky, paid with his life for his beliefs. With him twenty-three young writers, actors, and artists perished. Some were shot. Some were buried alive. Jou Shih was one of the latter.

Fourteen years later, at Kunming in October, 1945, there was a students' strike against the civil war. The strikers came from three of China's foremost universities—Peking, Tsinghua, and Nankai in Tientsin. Three students and a teacher were killed in the Kuomintang terror which followed. The leader of this demonstration was Wen Yi-tuo, a poet. He was no Communist, being only a Socialist of the type which Mr. Attlee would welcome and Mr. Bevan spurn. This was one of many nights of the long knives.

Most of China's intellectuals would have preferred a middle course avoiding both the mental tyranny of the Communists and the meaningless cruelties of the Kuomintang. Faced with a choice, they plumped for the Communists, but only as the lesser of two evils. In 1949 the Communists signified change—perhaps for the better.

Now they seemed less certain. Of the many things that impressed and repelled me during our stay in China nothing burned itself so strongly in my mind as the mental furtiveness of her intellectuals. In India during the British period I had often heard it said that the foreign rulers could imprison a man's body behind bars and barbed wires but they could not imprison his mind. In China I discovered that a man's mind could be chained, tethered, and imprisoned.

Why did these scholars whose intellect once had flowered in a free air fight shy of the very mention of Harvard, Princeton, Oxford, and Cambridge? I knew that many of them had been educated at one or another of these universities; and in their speech still lingered the accents of these academic centres.

The nimble Chinese mind delights in conversation. It loves nothing better than to prick and puncture the bubble of conceit. Less metaphysical than the Indian mind, it is more practical and more sensitive, prone to express itself in imagery and illustration, building an argument through suggestion rather than statement and weaving it in the "boneless way" of Huang Ch'uan, who painted birds, flowers, and gentle landscapes without a drawn outline.

In Kunming during the war I had talked with many professors

and students. We had sat for hours discussing many things, and always the tingle of their thought had delighted me. There was something in their quick, cerebral processes which, while Oriental, was also distinct. Their minds, tortured by tragedy, were often lit with laughter. And their conversation, gay, brittle, sensitive, and perceptive, had an elfin quality different from the Indian or the Japanese. It was as if a room were suddenly and softly illumined, and the lights dipped slowly again.

I tried to take up the threads. Something had snapped. They would not talk to you as of old. They murmured small polite pleasantries before sidling away. It was impossible to get them to speak in the language they once had employed. They echoed—sometimes faintly, sometimes assertively—the dicta of Communist China, mouthing the new jargon as children mouth the words of a new nursery rhyme.

For the first time I realised what for many years I had sensed vaguely but never grasped. To have your body imprisoned behind prison walls is degrading. But to have your mind captive with invisible chains is far more degrading. In the democratic beholder such a spectacle creates a pain and nausea difficult to describe or overcome.

Marxism, I knew, had long influenced the outlook of China's intellectuals, who for the most part were attracted by its theories of compassion and humanity without comprehending fully its more mechanistic implications. For them Marxism was an academic exercise. They saw it from afar through the gilded gauze of Soviet writing, which portrayed it as a fight against inequality and injustice. Here, many felt, was a brave new world far different from the violence and corruption of Kuomintang China. They had hoped for reform; but change was a distant mirage. And then Mao came like a new Moses, leading his millions to the Promised Land.

To travel is always more exciting than to arrive. Achievement had brought with it the promise of a new day, but dawn had dulled into darkness at noon. These intellectuals might not always have been able to speak aloud in Kuomintang China, but now they found that they could not even whisper. The old frustrations brought with them new fears. It made one slightly uncomfortable speaking to them and listening to their strangulated talk. Obviously they had never had any real contact with the masses. They had lived in a world of make-believe, and now another illusion was shattered. Like children, they seemed to be afraid to walk in the dark.

A man's thinking, say the Marxists, is influenced by his existence. His existence is not determined by his thinking. Many of China's intellectuals had thought otherwise. They had believed in art for art's sake. Dr. Kuo Mo-jo, China's leading litterateur, and one of the country's four Vice-Premiers, had travelled to Marx via Heine and Shelley. He had shared their belief until the middle twenties, when he had abandoned the formula of art for art's sake for the slogan of art for the people's sake. Even Dr. Hu Shih, a former president of Peita University, had taught that man's mind is determined by his society. But Hu Shih had fled the field while they remained.

Now their minds felt the compelling force of the society around them. San and Wu Fan—the drives against corruption, waste, and bribery—had their counterpart in the academic world. In schools and colleges the movement took an ideological, not economic, form. It borrowed the process of criticism and confession and applied it to educational ends. For more than five months normal work in the universities was virtually suspended while students and professors met in protracted sessions to criticise one another's deficiencies and probe and analyse their own. Our visit coincided with the last few weeks of this movement.

Opinion was divided. Some thought these sessions were remarkably good-tempered, and the foreign professors accepted them as part of the new order of things. Jain, an Indian professor of Hindi at Peking University, was enthusiastic.

"Far from creating a rift between students and professors," he remarked, "it has forged a new comradeship between us."

Others were less enthusiastic. An American professor of English was taken to task by his students for choosing "reactionary subjects," for their essays. The students insisted on setting the subjects. "Just now," said Panikkar, who told me the story, "germ warfare seems to be a popular subject."

In India, as in other democratic countries, the government passes a law when it wants something done. In China it starts a movement. San Fan derived directly from the government, and though launched in December, 1951, it was foreshadowed as far back as the previous August when the calculating, cold-blooded Kao Kang, Governor of Tung-pei, which is China's northeastern administrative zone, sounded the tocsin warning the Communists of corruption in their midst. In October Mao, addressing the third session of the People's Political Consultative Conference, which is China's temporary parliament, spoke of the "sugar-coated shells" of the capitalists or national bourgeoisie, who although one of the four friendly classes were, he said, infiltrating into and corrupting the government machine.

From Peking shortly after, the word went forth for a country-wide offensive. This was double-pronged. While directed initially against corrupt officials and party members it was designed to include the "contaminators," or commercial classes. The only difference between the San and Wu Fan movements was that the former was openly initiated by the government, while the latter apparently emanated from the penitent commercial classes. San Fan was confined to officials and party members. Wu Fan was restricted to the business community.

The extension of these movements into the student world was no spontaneous development. It was carefully planned. The "brain-washing," or ideological spring cleaning, which started in the universities was the juvenile counterpart of the adult and more drastic purges. Superficially it appeared to be a movement generated by the students and professors. In reality it was the climax to a long process of propaganda and indoctrination from above. Here was an interesting example of the Communist technique of making it appear as if the people themselves were taking the initiative in decisive action. Actually the government had set the machinery in motion.

It follows that all branches of Chinese education are permeated by this policy of thorough Marxist indoctrination, and all subjects are taught from the point of view of Marxist dogma and thought.

"Yes, we've altered the teaching of philosophy," said a Chinese professor of philosophy in answer to my question. "In the old days we paid no attention to the historical background of philosophical thought. We're revising our philosophy in the light of that background."

He was echoing the Communist view of the two factors which influence human conduct—mind and environment. In the Red reckoning the traditional philosophers had exaggerated the influence of the former and deprecated unduly the value of the latter.

The heads of most of the universities were not educationists but fervent party men. At the well-known Medical University of North China in Mukden the thirty-five-year-old president revealed himself as a veteran revolutionary who had not completed his course of formal medical training.

"But," he remarked, "I learned medicine under the supervision of foreign friends during the liberation war."

Later the president declared that the object of the Medical University was to train students "to realise the aims of revolutionary Communism." He went on to observe that the students were not taught, like pre-liberation doctors, "to serve only the privileged few; they had to serve the working class."

The library of this university contained some 100,000 books, including many English textbooks and magazines. Closer inspection revealed that most of them were out of date. The latest magazine was the *British Journal of Ophthalmology* of October, 1950. Presumably the bamboo curtain also screens the Communists' academic world. The building, incidentally, was constructed by the Japanese, and our guides described it as "enemy property."

Although every school and university is a Marxist breeding ground, certain institutes are exclusively dedicated to a drastic curriculum of indoctrination and training. Among these is the People's University at Peking, which we visited.

Here workers' and peasants' sons and daughters were trained as technicians, and for ultimate employment as officials. We were welcomed in a much beflagged hall, gay with slogans and posters, and sat down to tea with some of the professors and pupils. Most of the students lacked formal education; but those introduced to us—they were presumably hand-picked—seemed remarkably good types, keenly intelligent and not without a friendly charm of manner. In the corridors and campus were other students, less impressive in appearance, some of them obvious rural types who were probably more representative of their colleagues than our companions at the tea table.

They observed a Spartan regimen which entailed waking up in the morning at five and remaining on their toes for the whole of a crowded day which ended around half past nine. The period marked for leisure was denoted as "organised free activity." About four times a week they were exposed to intensive lectures and discussions, ranging over three or four hours, on subjects such as dialectic and historical materialism, the New Democracy, Chinese Communist history, and Mao Tse-tung's thought. These major sessions were supplemented by smaller group discussions.

Lack of trained personnel and the need for more doctors and technicians have led to the adoption of accelerated or shorter courses in schools and universities. The standard of university education, particularly in scientific studies, is disappointing. Laboratory equipment was generally poor and deficient while some academic centres suffered from a dearth of textbooks as these are only now being revised and rewritten in Chinese. With no foreign aid and few foreign experts, progress is hampered. Simultaneously the old avenues for foreign training have shrunk perceptibly.

Thrown largely upon their own resources, the Chinese are handling the problem courageously and with characteristic ingenuity. They are trying to make do with what they have. More than one scientist remarked wryly that the Chinese preferred a temporary lowering in efficiency to the presence of foreign experts. But they seemed to speak with no great conviction and with a latent sense of accepting the inevitable.

Two characteristics are noticeable in the country's academic life. Political hostility to the West is reflected in an intellectual xenophobia extending from students to professors. There is a marked reluctance to speak English even among those well versed in the language. On a visit to Nankai University a scientist colleague of mine, Dr. Bhagavantam, who is the head of the Physics Laboratory at Secunderabad, India, found great difficulty in conversing with the Dean through an interpreter who floundered badly over the technical terms. Bhagavantam was greatly taken aback when he discovered later that the Dean was a mathematics graduate of London University and spoke English fluently.

The other characteristic is the utilitarian bias which the new regime has injected into scientific studies. We passed an entire afternoon in the laboratories and workshops of the American-endowed Tsinghua University which now specialises in scientific and technical education. Here, as also at the North China Institute of Agricultural Research, the emphasis was on practical, applied work rather than on fundamental research.

Bhagavantam, remarking on this, observed: "In India, where we tend to be metaphysical, more work is being done in the realm of abstract, fundamental research. Here they concentrate on the applied uses of science. Of course, on the long-term basis science would not progress without fundamental research. China has gone to one extreme. We are in danger of going to the other."

The Communists lay great store by learning for practical ends. At the time of our visit the North China Institute was concentrating its research on millet and other food grains. The production of rinderpest vaccine was also actively under way. There appeared to be some liaison agency between the government and these institutes. Its job was to sift out immediate practical problems for research and pass them on for investigation to the institutes.

At Tsinghua was an American-trained mathematician of international standing. His subject was the theory of numbers. The government had left him free to carry on his research. "But," he confessed ruefully, "the overwhelming majority of students here is not interested in such abstract subjects."

China's scientists are keen on carrying the results of the laboratory to the fields and factories. There is about professors and students, more particularly the latter, a sense of bustle, of active and dedicated service to the State. But it is doubtful whether the regime as such is greatly concerned about or interested in university education or in the propagation of knowledge for knowledge's sake. It seemed to me that the government was keener on training its *kanpus,* or minor officials, through accelerated courses than on turning out university graduates.

We visited one such accelerated course high school in Peking. Here proletarian boys and girls, drawn from the strata of peasants, industrial workers, and soldiers came for a course of expedited studies before going to the university. They were obviously the pick of a miscellaneous bunch and took pride in having made the grade. In China the Stakhanovite principle operates in schools no less than in factories. The director introduced some of them to us, reciting a list of each one's achievements as peasant, worker, and soldier. Many of them wore ribbons on their suits and some sported medals, testimony to their prowess in the cause of increased production. Their demeanour impressed. They were modest but proud at having been singled out for individual mention and award. Watching them, I was better able to understand the Marxist method of attracting personal loyalty by giving each person an individual pride in collective achievement. Even if they were cogs in a vast machine, they were animated cogs whose individual contribution the State was ready to acknowledge and acclaim.

Through the maze of tangled episodes one incident comes back. Always shall I remember a morning in Mukden when I watched a "crocodile" of preternaturally solemn children marching four abreast down the street.

"Where are they going, Chang?" I asked our interpreter.

"To a picnic," he said. "It's a picnic procession."

I thought the phrase incongruous. A picnic procession? "Picnic" conjures up a process, hurried and haphazard, an occasion allowed to develop as the spirit wills it, bringing a vista of packed hampers, laughter and song, a winding road through green fields and hills, and a nook by a quiet stream.

Solemn children marching four abreast, marching to a picnic. Robots on the road. Sunlight and shadow. It was incongruous and absurd. It was also pathetic. But in those school children tramping solemnly to a picnic I think I saw briefly and in a flash the heart and mind of Mao's China.

4

"THE LAND IS OURS"

In Shansi in May the earth is green and gentle. As our train rolled westward from Peking we gazed on furrowed fields stretching far away to gay orchards and hills. The mud-thatched roofs of villages were brown-gold in the evening sun.

In the fading twilight we made a wayside halt. Over on the other side of the railway crossing was a peasant family on the way home from work. A child in blue was in the foreground. Seated on the ground were the mother, her head swathed in a white cloth, an older woman, presumably the grandmother, and two young peasants. Beside the group stood the farmer with his hoe, and between him and his family were three donkeys. A great immense bare tract of black soil sprawled behind them, and beyond were the green fields. It was like a painting by Corot.

Land is the crux of China's economic problem. With land are tied up the fortunes of city and countryside, industry and agriculture, politics and economics. Communist statistics are highly fluid and relative, but it is widely conceded that eight out of ten families in China's small towns and seven out of ten in the big cities have property links with the countryside. Since many landlords lived originally in the cities and many land-hungry peasants drifted for employment to the towns, the urban-rural links are intricate and intertwined. Even on the Kuomintang reckoning nearly 85 per cent of China's people subsist on the soil.

Mao's revolution was spearheaded by the peasantry, and though today he seeks to inflate the proletariat's role in the achievement of his millennium the peasantry is still the bedrock of his rule. If the Communist programme of land reform succeeds during the next decade it will change not only the economic but the political face of China.

Symbolism plays a large part in the mechanism of Marxist thought and action. By helping the peasants to eliminate the land-lords China's rulers hope to erase the image of feudalism, destroying at one stroke its economic and political power. Since Marxist vocabulary equates feudalism with imperialism, the destruction of one must help in the elimination of the other. In the Communist reckoning, by increasing the purchasing power of the rural areas it will be possible to step up the industrialisation of the towns. But simultaneously this process must create a property-conscious class of peasants which the regime might find it very difficult to eradicate later. In laying the ghost of feudalism the Communists may be creating the Frankenstein of a rich and possessive peasantry.

That, briefly, is the problem and paradox of China's land reforms. How are the Communists working it out?

In Kuomintang days money-making had centred largely on foodstuffs, particularly in the army commissariat. This partly accounted for the decline in industrial production because the returns on capital from industry were much lower than those from land. Hence the rapacity of the privileged classes was concentrated primarily on the peasants.

Mindful of the need to maintain if not increase production, and to carry all classes with them against the Japanese invader the Communists in the early stages refrained from confiscation and were content to reduce taxation and interest. During my wartime

visit to Chungking in 1944 I had often heard my colleagues in
the Press Hostel refer to the Communists as "agrarian reformers."
Even a Russian journalist representing Tass who had visited Mao
Tse-tung's headquarters in Yenan described the situation in that
area to me as one of "peaceful Communism."

"They've even got merchants and landlords represented in the
border governments," he remarked.

This was true. Except for the more notorious pro-Japanese,
landowners were not often dispossessed by the Communists, although some landless peasants were given waste land for cultivation. Generally, at this stage, the Communist authorities bought a
certain percentage of agricultural produce, leaving landlord and
farmer free to sell the rest at controlled rates. Everyone had to
work and produce. Rent had always weighed heavily on the
farmer. "A straw cape in the rain," he called it. "The longer you
wear it, the heavier it becomes." The peasant's rent was now
reduced from the original 60 to 70 per cent of his crop so that
he was liable to the landlord only for about 30 per cent. On the
other hand, the Yenan government of those days mulcted its subjects by taxation ranging from 3 to 35 per cent. Apart from col-
lecting tax and grain there was Communist currency in the shape
of border region bank notes.

This deceptive and highly idealised state of affairs, confined
to those areas of North China which the Communists controlled,
ended abruptly in May, 1946, when the Communist party decided
to change its programme of rent and interest reductions to one
of confiscating the landlords' estates and distributing them among
the peasants. This policy was partly implemented in North and
Northeast China and in Shantung province between 1946 and
1948. About half of the land in Manchuria and North China was
redistributed after expropriating the holdings of some 15 per cent
of the population.

At this stage no distinction appears to have been made between
the landlords and the "rich" peasants. A "rich" peasant's holdings

averaged from eight to ten acres of land while a landlord's holdings were generally in the neighbourhood of 45 acres. Initially both categories had their land impounded, and by June, 1949, some 15,000,000 out of a total of 100,000,000 farmers and landlords in widespread areas of North China and Manchuria were deprived of their holdings. Some believe that in this period about 500,000 individuals were executed for "feudal crimes."

In June, 1950, Mao, submitting his first report on the state of the nation, heralded another shift in the Communists' agrarian programme. "There must be a change," he declared, "in our attitude towards the rich peasant. We must no longer requisition surplus land and the property of the rich peasants. We must preserve our rich peasant economy, for nothing matters so much as the restoration of production in the rural areas."

That same month the Central People's Government, which had been proclaimed in Peking only eight months earlier, promulgated the new Land Reform Law. In August of the same year the Government Administration Council of the central government announced the "Decisions Concerning the Differentiation of Class Status in the Countryside," explaining therein the various classes or categories in the countryside. These comprised landlords, rich peasants, middle peasants, poor peasants, and hired labourers.

China's land reforms as I saw them are governed largely by these two enactments. Significantly the shift in agrarian policy came with the strengthening of political status. It now became necessary to increase agricultural output with a view to achieving economic stability and consolidating the government's fiscal position. The Communists calculate that with a rise in rural production must come a rise in rural purchasing power. This, they believe, will ultimately provide a broad and solid base for China's industrialisation. The basic aim of agrarian reform, says China's Marxist high priest, Liu Shao-chi, is not alone relieving the poor peasants. Agrarian reform is primarily the condition precedent to the development of the country's productive power and to its industrialisation. In the ultimate analysis China's industrialisation hinges on the vastness of her rural markets.

Shortly after our arrival in Peking we visited our first land reform village, some five miles outside the city walls. We motored there, branching after a while off the main highway and riding over a rough, dusty country road which wound amid a patchwork of grey-green fields. Not all of the land was cultivated.

As our cavalcade of cars swung to a stop we were greeted by what appeared to be a considerable portion of the village population. Grubby, cheerful children smiled a welcome and clapped hands. Sturdy peasant women, their broad, weatherbeaten faces creased in smiles, came eagerly forward, linking hands easily with the women members of our delegation. The gnarled fists of stocky, genial peasants closed over ours. It was friendly and pleasant.

I felt an odd communion with these simple folk, who like children with new toys were obviously eager to show us their possessions. Their pride in what they had was unsophisticated and contagious. This farmer had a pig and five hens. That lucky fellow had a donkey. They opened chests to show us quilted suits. Some of their houses had radio sets, obviously part of the "surplus assets" of the twenty landlords who once had owned the larger part of the village fields. Garish vases stood on shelves alongside a few quieter pieces of porcelain or pottery. Pictures adorned some of the walls.

In this village of about forty families totalling some two hundred persons, the average individual holding was a little under two mus, or less than one-third of an acre of land; but each member of a family, including infants, had his or her share. The average family holding was about eight mus, or an acre and a third.

This is true generally of Hopeh, the province including Peking. But holdings differ with the pressure of population on the land. In the Northeast, in Manchuria, where the density of population is comparatively low, the average individual holding is about three mus, or half an acre. Below Hopeh in the south it tapers off to 1.5 mus per head.

Some of us were curious to know the present status of the dispossessed landlords.

The village spokesman explained. He was evidently a trained cadre or trusted party official on whom devolved the task of initiating land reform in the village. He bristled with facts and figures.

The landlords, he told us, though dispossessed were given shares of land equal to those of the peasants. That was indeed so. But they had no share in the administrative councils of the village, since this carried the right to vote. The landlords were deprived of civic rights for periods depending on their capacity and willingness to reform. They also had no share in the benefits of the village cooperative canteen, where prices for basic goods were 10 per cent lower than in the open market.

In the Marxist political cupboard everything and everybody is neatly labelled, docketed, and defined.

What, we asked, was the definition of "landlord"?

The village spokesman launched on another lengthy dissertation. Landlords, he explained, had been a small minority who did not work on their land, got others to till it, and exacted from them excessive rent and interest. They had also often worked as tax collectors. Thus they had controlled rent, interest, prices, and taxes. Before the land reforms the landlords constituted only 5 per cent of the rural population and owned 50 to 60 per cent of all agricultural land in the country.

Actually, as we discovered on probing further, "landlord" in Communist China covers individuals holding eight to forty-five acres and more. Thus the "rich" peasants who partly worked their land themselves and partly hired labour to do it held per head eight to ten acres of land. Many among them rented out part of their land, and some practised usury. On the Communist reckoning, the "rich" peasants owned about 10 per cent of the arable land in China. In other words, the landlords and rich peasants, who between them constituted some 10 per cent of the rural population, owned 70 per cent or more of the land.

"Is the rich peasant," I asked, "allowed to keep his land?"

"As a general rule, yes," said the village spokesman; "but in certain special areas the land rented out by him may be requisitioned in part or in whole. This is done with the approval of the people's governments at a provincial or higher level."

He went on to explain another significant fact. Certain landowners, he said, belong to the class of revolutionary army men or professional people who own and rent out small plots of land. These are allowed to retain twice the average per capita holding in their area.

"Always remember," he said, "that our object is to step up agricultural production and promote industrialisation. Therefore, even in the case of a landlord, we are careful to distinguish between the feudal and nonfeudal parts of his property. Industrial and commercial enterprises operated by a landlord are exempt from confiscation. So are the land and other properties which he uses directly for running industrial and commercial ventures. Thus large farms, if run on capitalist lines, are allowed to continue functioning. And the owner may keep all of his equipment."

We explored our catechism further.

"What is a middle peasant?" somebody inquired.

A middle peasant in the Red dictionary is one who tills the land himself and can generally subsist on his own labour. Going down the scale, a poor peasant is one whose land is insufficient for his upkeep. Hence he is compelled to hire out his own labour as a harvest hand or a day worker. Lowest in the scale stands the hired labourer, who, having no land, ekes his existence from the sweat of his brow.

"You understand our land reforms, don't you?" said the village spokesman, having explained the background. "Between them the middle and poor peasants and hired labourers constitute 90 per cent of our rural population. Before the land reforms they collectively owned 30 per cent or less of the land."

The main impulse and incentive for the land reforms come from the poor peasants and hired labourers. Naturally the regime regards them as the core of the movement and hopes by uniting them with the middle peasants to isolate the landlord class and neutralise ultimately the rich peasants. But for the present, until the time is ripe for the climax of collectivisation, the rich peasant is tolerated.

Thus the same motive force which impels temporary recognition of the capitalist class as a friendly category within the industrial structure compels a similar attitude to the rich peasant and even to the "nonfeudal" landlord on the agrarian plane. Both are vital concomitants to increased output. Like Stalin, Mao zigzags to his target.

China's land reforms provide another illustration of the regime's technique of appearing to associate the people with the government's activities whereas actually the initiative and direction come from the party. When the government decides that land in a village should be parcelled out among the peasants it sends three or four of its trained party officials into the village. Earlier the ground has been prepared by the removal of what the Communists describe as "rural despots." The peasants have also previously been encouraged to reduce rents and reclaim their advance deposits, which normally total some 60 to 70 per cent of their crop. In the process local Peasants' Associations are organised, and the visiting party officials operate largely through them.

These officials propagate the idea that the land belongs by right to the peasants. The gospel catches on. Accusation meetings are held where the landlords' iniquities are denounced. The landlords are then dispossessed, and the peasants "come into their own." This happens only after a careful definition of the class status of the village people has been made. Under the guidance of the cadres the status of each individual in the village is carefully defined, determined, and tabulated, and the number of landlords, of rich peasants, middle peasants, poor peasants, and hired labourers is worked out and announced. Each of the first three categories is deprived of its "surplus assets," and each of the five classes then receives its precise basic share of land and equipment.

Two paradoxes emerge from this parcelling-out process. Although the division between the five classes is theoretically eliminated unequal holdings persist in practice while the sense of property is preserved. How to escape from this self-created dilemma is the major problem of China's land reformers.

According to Communist statistics, some 130,000,000 rural people were affected by the reforms during 1951. Earlier, in the old liberated areas such as Manchuria, North China, and Shantung, another 190,000,000 peasants had been benefited, making a total of 320,000,000 rural people, or 80 per cent of all who live in the Chinese countryside. In 1952 the Communists claimed that the land reforms extended to the entire Chinese mainland with the exception of certain regions inhabited by the national minorities. In these racial pockets concentrated largely in the Southwest and the Northwest reside some 25,000,000 of the country's 475,000,000 people. Here the land reforms will be introduced only when "the majority of the masses among the minorities demand it." That this demand will be manipulated from above by the party when the time is ripe is certain.

Already the progress of the land reforms has propelled into being an army of more than 300,000 cadres, or trained officials dedicated to this specific task. They, not the peasantry, form the spearhead of the rural revolution which in its stride has liquidated nearly two million "counter-revolutionaries," "rural despots," and "feudal landlords." On the agrarian as on most other fronts the voice is to all appearances the voice of the people, but the hand is the hand of the party.

If differing pressures of population compel varied patterns of land distribution ranging from 1.5 mus per head in the south to

3 mus per head in Manchuria the pace of progress on the land also varies. Broadly, agrarian reform as the Communists visualise it runs in three stages. The parcelling-out of land is followed by the organisation of agricultural production through two processes. The preliminary process consists of the forming of mutual aid teams and setting up production cooperatives. Stemming from these two stages is the third and final stage of collectivisation of agriculture on the pattern of collective farming in the Soviet Union.

China's land reforms struggle at varied tempos through the mutual aid and cooperative stages. Collectivisation, still to be achieved, was a nebulous, distant goal until mid-1951, when significantly it crept often and more aggressively into high-level party pronouncements and speeches. China is now in the "creeping collectivisation" stage.

Under the mutual aid system a peasant joins a mutual aid team and tills his land with the aid of his associates' labour, draft cattle, and farm equipment. In turn he lends similar aid when other members of his team requisition help. Although a cooperative spirit is thereby engendered, the system is individualistic enough to permit each peasant to grow whatever he chooses on his land and this sometimes makes for unproductive output. The system, which has two manifestations—temporary mutual aid teams and permanent mutual aid teams—is prevalent in South and Central China. It was a feature of the Hopeh village near Peking which we visited.

In a temporary mutual aid team little more than short-term pooling of labour during the busy seasons is involved. A permanent mutual aid team is generally an aggregation of several temporary teams; and under its aegis tools, draft animals, and labour are pooled. Both systems, though worked by the peasants, are directed by a party cadre, who is generally but not always a party member. When not a party member he none the less takes his orders from the party. In the Hopeh village this personage was referred to euphemistically as a commissioner of civil affairs, and might, for all we knew, have been the village spokesman who conducted us around.

Statistics are as hard to come by in China as a white elephant in Siam. When available they are usually cited in terms of percentages, very rarely in terms of absolute quantities or figures. In the Hopeh village the spokesman entranced us with a long, quick-fire recitation of percentages without reference to a note. His was obviously a command performance.

Production, he claimed, had been stepped up over the past two years; and he buttressed this by a list of percentages. Broken down into specific figures by dint of querying it appeared that the average annual share or gross income of each family, though assessed in terms of basic commodities or catties (1 catty = 1.2 pounds) of rice, was valued at a little over a thousand dollars. Of this each family had contributed an average of twenty dollars to the Aid Korea Resist America Fund. Government taxes are paid in grain, and the figure given us varied with localities. Broadly it appeared to be 18 to 27 per cent of the produce in a normal year. Some proportion of the gross income was laid aside for a kind of common sinking fund, and the farmer was free to sell the remainder of his produce after providing for his own and his family's needs. Purchase and sale are transacted through cooperative agencies.

The common sinking fund is one of the principal leading strings which hold the peasantry to the regime. By stepping up the farmer's contribution to this fund and increasing official taxes or "voluntary" contributions the administration can regulate the peasant's individual earnings. Moreover the fact that some of his income is tied up in the sinking fund gives a collective edge to the farmer's individual efforts.

What impressed me was the keen sense of property among the peasants. This was particularly noticeable in the land reform village we visited farther north, near Mukden in Manchuria. It was a larger village than the one in Hopeh and was in a more advanced state of reform. It was a production cooperative village covering some 450 acres of which 88 per cent, according to our guide, was formerly held by eight landlord families.

Unlike the Hopeh project, which was initiated in 1950, this Manchurian village started on land reform as far back as 1948. The mutual aid team stage was a thing of the past. The production cooperative process was now under way.

Membership in the production cooperatives, we were told, was voluntary. Of the 166 adults in the village, 125 were members. Landlords were not admitted since membership in cooperatives carried the right to vote. Oddly enough, the principle of property was respected, even stressed, under this system. In production cooperatives the individual farmer invests not only his equipment, cattle, and labour but his land in the common pool. This distinguishes them from the mutual aid teams. Another distinction is that in production cooperatives the land is cultivated on a collective, areawise, not individual basis. The number and variety of crops to be sown are determined jointly by the members of the cooperatives, who assess the matter on a strictly economic reckoning.

When the crops are harvested a due proportion is set aside for payment of government taxes. Next, a certain amount is earmarked for the purchase of seeds for the following year's sowing. The remainder is then divided among the members in proportion to their investment of labour, land, cattle, and equipment. Labour, assessed according to men-days of work, absorbed 60 per cent while land yielded 30 per cent and cattle and equipment 10 per cent. The significant point about this tabulation is the low share of proceeds earmarked for land as compared to labour. As with mutual aid teams, members of the cooperatives are required to make various "voluntary" contributions to funds, organisational and governmental.

Yet undeniably the peasants of this Manchurian village were imbued with a sense of property and progress. One of the most interesting features of our visit was a talk with a model worker. He stood in his blue jeans, a sturdy farmer with a seamed, strong face. His wife, a lively, capable woman, joined spiritedly in the conversation. They had a six-year-old daughter. The three lived in a mud hut of two rooms, both kept scrupulously clean though this might conceivably have been for our benefit. On one of the walls hung a print of General Chu Teh.

Between them these three owned nine mus—one and a half acres. The man supplemented his income with a handcart which carried farm produce. Occasionally he did other odd jobs such as helping to build houses. These chores earned him an additional 3,000,000 yuans (approximately $150) per year. His wife reared pigs and poultry. She sold eggs and sometimes a pig.

"We have three pigs and eighteen hens," said the woman proudly.

I was greatly struck by their quiet pride in property. Like peasants the world over, they were simple but shrewd folk.

I asked the farmer if he was happier now than he had been under the Kuomintang regime.

"Why shouldn't I be?" he answered. "Then I was a landless labourer. Now we have our nine mus of land, this hut, and"—his eyes swept out of the open window—"our hens and pigs and cattle. I have also my handcart."

"What happens when the land is collectivised?"

He shrugged his shoulders. "We shall still have our share of the produce. And production will increase."

Did he mean what he said? Or would he later look back nostalgically to the days that were and might still be? It is difficult to read a man's mind in Mao's China.

Here as in other land reform villages the children went to school, and as we left the village they came to cheer us on our way, waving flags and singing songs. They were rubicund and robust. Unlike Indian children, Chinese youngsters are by no means shy and self-conscious. Small pink paws were stretched out for the inevitable handshake, and they clustered around us, eager, friendly, enthusiastic, and inquisitive. It was impossible to resist them.

"In the old days," said our guide, "only twenty children—most of them the landlords' children—went to school. Now we have ninety-six."

The adult peasants also work to liquidate their own illiteracy. In farms as in factories production is stimulated by individual competition, which brings its rewards in medals and titles for model workers.

The women too seemed emancipated. Child marriage was officially frowned upon. The legal age for marriage is now eighteen for girls and twenty for men. From what we were told it seemed as if those women who were wedded under the old laws as children have, if they choose, a right to divorce.

Medical aid was also dispensed, a medical base serving a group of villages through mobile relief vans. Midwives of the old school were gradually being educated to new ways. So at least we were assured.

About these land reform villages was an air of progress and prosperity. Pervading them was the peasants' strong and growing sense of property. This has not escaped the eyes of an ever-watchful regime.

Although, as Mao proclaimed as far back as 1943, "the only road to collectivisation, according to Lenin, is through cooperatives," the Communist rulers of modern China recognise that both the mutual aid teams and the production cooperatives provide fruitful soil for the inculcation of a sense of property. In a speech in January, 1952, Kao Kang, the powerful Governor of Tung-pei, or Northeast China (which includes Manchuria), complained of certain elements who "consider it their responsibility after economic conditions have improved to lead the hired farm labourers to the status of rich peasants, giving them something to look forward to."

Clearly this was anathema. "This," said Kao Kang, "is to make the working class forsake its leadership towards the peasants. This is to surrender to the growth of capitalism in the rural villages and to let the peasants develop spontaneously until they become rich peasants, or to let the poor peasants sink down as their economic conditions deteriorate. In short, this is to let our rural villages tread the path of capitalism."

Hence the revived urge for collectivisation which found expression in mid-1951 in a directive to accelerate the agrarian programme in all its phases. According to an article written in November, 1951, by Wu Chueh-nung, Vice Minister of Agriculture, the total number of production cooperatives throughout China was over 200 at the time, and there were nearly 100 in North China. Since then they have increased greatly; and in April, 1952, the New China News Agency, quoting certain instructions by Kao Kang, gave their total as over 1,200.

To lead the peasants gradually towards collectivisation the government has more recently set up model State farms—one report mentions more than 500 in Manchuria alone—where the peasants might see for themselves the "benefits" of collectivisation. We heard of these vaguely but saw none.

China's first two collective farms were reported in the Communist press in the summer of 1952. One is said to be near Kiamusze in Sungkiang province in northeastern Manchuria; the other, near Tihwa in Sinkiang province. But in the more densely populated agricultural areas, particularly in East China, it is doubtful whether conditions will be ripe for collectivisation for some years to come. Recognising this, the Communist plan is to hasten slowly. At the same time any drift towards "rural complacency" and any move away from collectivisation to "selfish" ideas of personal enrichment are being vigilantly watched. The primary task of the farmer, it is emphasized, is to increase production—not in order "to become rich" but "to benefit the nation." The agricultural tax is described as "a glorious burden."

Because the old Adam in man will never be rooted out voluntarily, it is inevitable that the acceptance by all farmers of the new way of life will be compulsory. The entire rural society is being brought into absolute subservience to the State. The government's primary aim is to increase its grip on the peasant and his produce. In short, the regime is slowly manoeuvring for the kill.

Meanwhile, by a mixture of blandishments and threats, the administration is partly inducing, partly pushing the peasants along the collectivist road. An independent peasantry with growing economic strength is a potential threat to the Communist State. The ideal is a docile, economically dependent rural population under close party control.

On the agrarian, as on the industrial, front China is in the penultimate stage of Communist development. With the achievement of complete Communism the capitalist will disappear from industry, and the peasant will no longer own his land, which will be the property of the State.

It is interesting to see the parallel approach to the businessmen and the peasants. Under full socialism, writes Liu Shao-chi, the capitalists can still serve the Communist State as "managers of socialist enterprises"; and their children, if trained now, could in time be employed as technical experts. The same promise is dangled before the peasants. "It is possible," writes Wu Chueh-nung, "that the leaders of the present mutual aid teams and agricultural cooperatives may become chairmen of collective farms or superintendents of State farms in the future."

Absolute statistics are lacking, so that it is difficult to assess the productive yield of the land reforms. The Communists claim self-sufficiency in food and all manner of other achievements. They remark on the increased purchasing power of the peasantry. An oft-quoted village saying runs: "One year after the land reform we can eat well; two years afterwards we can buy new equipment; in three years we will be well-to-do." But that, the Communists' own utterances indicate, is precisely the fear which haunts the regime.

One heard fabulous stories of the purchases which the new-rich farmers were making. A popular story tells of an East China farmer, head of a family of four, who after a single harvest bought a bicycle, a Thermos flask, and six electric torches.

"And what do four people want to do with six electric torches?" inquired a neighbour.

"My daughter-in-law," said the farmer, "is expecting twins."

The problem of China's land reforms runs in a vicious circle. Greater production means larger income for the peasant and bigger purchasing power for the countryside. This means the regrowth of a class of purse-proud, property-conscious peasants who with time must ossify into a vested interest hostile to any appropriatory or expropriatory measures.

On the other hand, can production really increase under the cumulative pressure of population and the growing fragmentation of land which must follow in its wake? Unless light and heavy industries supplemented by tertiary services, such as communications and the professional services of doctors and teachers, grow, pressure on the land is bound to intensify with resulting surplus labour. In the North, where the population is less densely spread, the extension of cooperatives is possible with no great dislocation of the rural economy; but in the East and South any large-scale extension can only result in more unemployment.

The Communists say that the answer to this is increased industrialisation. But have they the capital means to effect it? Moreover they themselves rely on a larger rural market to absorb their greater industrial output, and the first is possible only if the purchasing power of the peasantry is stepped up by a larger income surplus. This would create the vested rural interest they dread and would complete the vicious circle.

Collectivisation is the Communist way out. Over China's peasantry, now increasingly aware that the illusive world it lives in must vanish like a feckless dream, hangs this ever-present menace. The hammer-and-sickle flag waves over the land reform villages. But behind the shadow of the flag is the scythe of the Grim Reaper who will soon slit their thin-spun thread of hope.

5

RULERS OF CHINA

In a remote village of Manchuria peasant girls looked in round-eyed wonder at us and asked if it were true that we had seen "Chairman Mao."

We assured them we had. Had he talked to us? Yes. And had he shaken hands with us? Even so. Then would we shake hands with them? Gladly we gave them their vicarious thrill.

Already in his lifetime Mao Tse-tung is a legend in his land. Throughout China, in cities, towns, and tiny villages, posters and prints carry the bland homely countenance of the man who sits in the seat of the Manchus at Peking. To millions of his countrymen and countrywomen Mao represents the Benign Father, the Great Provider, the dispenser of all bounties and blessings.

After the May Day parade at which we first saw him Mao walked to each corner of the yellow-tiled pavilion where he stood with his praetorian guard and doffed his cap in salutation to the crowds. I thought how much he looked like the pictures, with his massive head of jet-black hair. The sun shone on him and, as he threw his head back in a gesture faintly regal, lighted up the broad familiar features.

Behind him, like a group of acolytes, trailed the trinity which in the Chinese mind symbolises the core of Mao's regime. There was General Chu Teh with his thick-set frame, his heavy hand rising occasionally in salute. The impassive Liu Shao-chi moved like a wan wraith in the shadows. Contrasting strongly with these two was the dapper figure of Chou En-lai, who plays the mandarin to Mao's peasant. Chou's tufted eyebrows were prominent, and he smiled often.

With Mao these three men sit in lofty eminence. They rule China.

The framework of the country's governmental structure was set up in Peking in September, 1949—eight months after the Communists entered it—by the Chinese People's Political Consultative Conference, more commonly known as the C.P.P.C.C. This conference, officially described as "the organisation of the democratic united front of the entire Chinese people," was attended by 622 delegates chosen by various regional, military, occupational, and racial groups, thus conforming broadly to the Soviet pattern. Besides the Communists, other political parties which had broken away from the Kuomintang were allowed representation. But "reactionary elements" were rigorously excluded.

The non-Communist elements are groups or cliques rather than parties; and, because acceptance of the Common Programme with its Marxist basis is a prerequisite for recognition and acceptance, these groups, for all practical purposes, toe the party line. Among them are the Revolutionary Committee of the Kuomintang, headed by Li Chi-shen; the China Democratic League, whose chairman is Chang Lan; the China Democratic National Construction Association; the China Association for Promoting Democracy; and the China Peasants and Workers Democratic Party.

A recent report suggests the virtual liquidation of the last-named group, but the probability is that it died a natural death. In any case, it is extremely doubtful if any of these non-Communist groups has any strong separate corporate existence. While we were in China we heard reports of Communist efforts to prop up some of those in danger of withering away from sheer inanition.

The C.P.P.C.C., besides adopting the Common Programme, elected the Central People's Government of the People's Republic of China, with Mao Tse-tung as its chairman. Officially this body is known as the Central People's Government Council, or C.P.G.C.; and it comprises, besides Mao, six vice-chairmen and 56 members. Of the vice-chairmen three—Chu Teh, Liu Shao-chi, and Kao Kang—are members of the Communist party. Chang Lan of the China Democratic League and Li Chi-shen of the Revolutionary Committee of the Kuomintang are the fourth and fifth. The sixth, Soong Ching-ling, the widow of Dr. Sun Yat-sen and the sister of Madame Chiang Kai-shek, has collaborated closely with the Communists for many years.

The C.P.G.C., which is the fount of authority, rules through four subordinate agencies. These are the Government Administration Council, the highest executive body for State administration, which approximates to the Western concept of a cabinet; the People's Revolutionary Military Council, which is the top-ranking organ of military command in the State; the Supreme People's Court, the highest judicial body; and the People's Procurator-General's Office, which has supreme supervisory power to ensure the strict observance of the law by all government institutions and public functionaries as well as by the people and nationals of the country. (The Common Programme distinguishes between people and nationals. The former comprise the four friendly classes—industrial workers, peasants, the petty bourgeoisie, and the national bourgeoisie. The latter, who are deprived of most civil and property rights until they reform, consist of the three unfriendly classes: the landlords, the anti-government Kuomintang "reactionaries," and the bureaucratic capitalists—that is, officials who have exploited their position in order to amass wealth.)

Communists head all but one of the four subordinate agencies.

Chou En-lai, Premier and Minister for Foreign Affairs, presides over the Government Administration Council, or cabinet. As the chief executive organ it controls four subcommittees: Political and Legal Affairs; Financial and Economic Affairs; Cultural and Educational Affairs; and People's Control. The last-named supervises the work of government institutions and public functionaries, and six men—the Premier, four Vice-Premiers, and the General Secretary—hold the key posts in the administration. Only two of them—the poet Kuo Mo-jo and Huang Yen-pei—are non-Communists. The Council supervises, besides these four subcommittees, about thirty subordinate ministries, commissions, academies, and administrations.

The second of the subordinate agencies, the People's Revolutionary Military Council, is headed by Mao Tse-tung; and Lo Jung-huan, member of the Central Committee of the Communist Party, is People's Procurator-General. The only non-Communist at the head of a key agency is Shen Chun-ju, the President of the Supreme People's Court, whose diminutive stature and wispy beard suggest one of Snow White's seven dwarfs. Shen, a veteran jurist, is a non-party man who is content to dispense the law as the Communists ordain.

China's Central Government is thus very much "centralised." As far back as June, 1945, Liu Shao-chi expounded to the Seventh Congress of the Communist party of China at Yenan *min-chu ti chi-chung chih-tu,* or "democratic centralism." Under this system, which is reminiscent in its contradictory connotation of the "people's democratic dictatorship," members of the party are bound to follow unconditionally the dictates of the Central Committee. This presumably ensures "centralism." The democratic element supposedly stems from the fact that the Committee is elected by the party congress; but the congress may not in fact be convened for years. For instance, seventeen years elapsed between the Sixth Congress in 1928 and the Seventh Congress in 1945, though the party constitution of 1945 now provides that the Congress shall be convened once every three years. The Central Committee may postpone these sessions of the Congress, so that the proviso is an expression of intention more than of fact. In other words, democracy operates only at the will of the central authority. This would seem to be the real meaning of "democratic centralism."

The principle of "democratic centralism" which is applicable to party affairs is now transferred to governmental matters. Authority is centralised in the Central People's Government Council, to whom all branches of the State apparatus—administrative, military, judicial, and supervisory—are responsible. On the analogy of the central committee, which must render account to the Communist party congress, the Central People's Government Council is responsible to the Chinese People's Political Consultative Conference. This relationship will last until the All China People's Congress, which will be convened on the basis of universal franchise, replaces the Conference. The responsibility for summoning this Congress rests on the Government Council, which the Organic Laws stipulate shall "prepare for and convene a conference of representatives of the entire nation." Not until the transitional period of welding China into a New Democracy is safely bridged will this be done. How long it will take is anyone's guess. Nineteen years elapsed between Chiang Kai-shek's promise of a convention in 1927 and its fulfilment in 1946.

The Communists' transitional period may conceivably be speedier, for the summoning of the People's Congress hinges on the accomplishment of a defined programme; and with the achievement of that target the regime will be more strongly entrenched than it now is, and the pattern of national life more firmly fixed. Land will be ready for collectivisation, and the capitalist will be reconciled to merging his identity in a classless society. From the present phase of a mixed economy China, so the Communists calculate, will move to State capitalism and eventually to Socialism. It is as if the stage were set for a drama where all the principal parts have been assigned to the actors and the denouement, being known to all, is planned and inevitable.

Between plenary sessions of the C.P.P.C.C., if and when they are called, a National Committee operates to supervise the execution of the Conference's resolutions and handle the daily routine. The Committee has 198 members, of whom until recently 180 were elected by the Conference. The other 18 still remain to be filled. In turn, the National Committee is assisted by a Standing Committee which includes Mao Tse-tung, Liu Shao-chi, Chu Teh, Chou En-lai, Li Chi-sen, and Chang Lan. Thus the chief personalities of the Central People's Government Council find places in the principal functional committee of the Chinese People's Political Consultative Conference. Caesar appeals unto Caesar.

Not since the golden days of the Manchu Emperors Kang Hsi and Chien Lung, whose reigns covered the greater part of the eighteenth century, have a government's decrees extended so firmly over the country as they do today. The Communists have been fortunate in two things. In the two decades over which their internal struggle was spread they forged not only an army but the framework of an administrative system. Thus they were able to take over the entire country, man its administration, and place behind it the effective sanction of military force.

The principle which keeps the government and the administrative machinery at the centre close-knit to the party extends over the entire country. China is divided today into six administrative areas, all except one administered by soldiers.

Tung-pei, the Northeast area, including Manchuria, is under a civilian. He is Kao Kang, one of the six Vice-Chairmen of the Central People's Government Council, and he rates high in the councils of the party. Tung-pei, abutting on Korea, includes the provinces of Sungkiang, Kirin, Heilungkiang, Liaotung, Liaosi, and Jehol and the Port Arthur and Dairen region, with a population of nearly 42,000,000. It also contains four cities, Mukden, Penki, Anshan, and Fushun.

The Northwest area, sprawling from the yellow hills of Shensi to the wastes of the Takla Makan Desert and beyond, is under General Peng Teh-huai. Peng, who comes from Mao's home province of Hunan and is close to Chu Teh, has a pronounced political consciousness. He holds that a soldier's morale is strong when he knows why he fights. He is also a great believer that an army can operate effectively only with the support of the people. The Northwest area is the base of the First Field Army and has a population of nearly 24,000,000. It comprises the provinces of Shensi, Kansu, Ningsia, Tsinghai, and Sinkiang along with the city of Sian.

General Jao Shu-shih rules over the East China area, along the coastal bulge, embracing the provinces of Kiangsu, Chekiang, Anhwei, Fukien, Shantung, and (theoretically) Formosa, with a population of nearly 141,000,000. Here are the two important cities of Shanghai and Nanking. A key figure in this region is the Mayor of Shanghai, General Chen Yi, commander-in-chief of the Third Field Army. Chen Yi, a genial, impressive figure, once led the famous Communist New Fourth Army.

The well-known General Lin Piao, commander-in-chief of the Fourth Field Army which at the end of 1950 was in action against the United Nations in Korea, heads the Central China and South China areas. Lin Piao, who is rated China's best military theorist, is simultaneously commander of the Central China military area, secretary of the regional Communist party bureau, and chairman of the area's Financial and Economic Committee. Although only forty-four he ranks very high in the party hierarchy. His charge includes his home province of Hupeh, Hunan, Honan, Kiangsi, Kwangtung, Kwangsi, and the cities of Canton and Hankow, with nearly 137,000,000 people. Canton's Mayor, one of the up-and-coming figures of the regime, is the capable, handsome, and suave General Yeh Chien-ying, who was at one time chief of staff of the Communist armies.

Another distinguished soldier, General Liu Po-cheng, administers the Southwest area, containing Szechwan, Kweichow, Yunnan, Sikang, and the city of Chungking, with a population of 70,000,000. Like General Chu Teh whom he once served as chief of staff, Liu comes from Szechwan. He was trained at the Red Academy in Moscow. In 1947 Liu headed the first Communist army which counterattacked the Kuomintang in China proper. Today he commands the Second Field Army, which "liberated" Tibet. He has the reputation of a daring tactician. With Lin Piao he forms the two military arms— strategic and tactical—of Chu Teh. The political fist is provided by General Peng Teh-huai, head of the Northwest area. Also in this region is the sixty-five-year-old General Ho Lung, another Hunanese, who as chief of staff serves under the youthful Liu. Ho, whose active soldiering days are over, is a member of the party's Revolutionary Military Affairs Committee.

One area—North China—has been directly under the Central Government since October 31, 1949. But General Nieh Jung-chen, chief of the Fifth Field Army, is said to wield considerable local influence as commander of the North China military area. Nieh led the Central Army when Mao struck back after being forced out of Yenan in March, 1947.

Outside the category of the six areas proper is the Inner Mongolian autonomous region with a population of 2,000,000. Its chairman is Ulanfu, a member of the Central People's Government Council.

Two men in China, not too well-known outside it, are worth watching. One is Kao Kang, the strong, surly, spectacled ruler over Manchuria—an unprepossessing individual with a pockmarked face, said to be devoid of most graces and manners. He is a Communist caricature come to life. Inflexible in purpose, inexorable in action, he tends to treat all outside his charmed circle with ill concealed disdain. But the man is able. Kao Kang rang the tocsin heralding the San Fan movement. In August,

1951, he foreshadowed a purge in an address to the party leaders of Manchuria. Soon after, he struck. Cold-blooded and calculating, he has the reputation of pursuing his ends with the dedicated remorselessness of a one-track mind. Although now head of the key zone of Tung-pei, his eyes rove towards Peking. Some day he may get there. Already he is one of China's six Vice-Chairmen.

The other man is Peng Chen. Peng combines a pugnacious countenance with great geniality of manner. Today he is Peking's Mayor and a member of the Central Committee of his party. Like Kao Kang, he was also prominent in the San Fan movement. He spoke to me about it one day after dinner, making his points directly, and his quick, compelling smile punctuated the recital. As mild-mannered a man, I thought, as ever scuttled ship or slit a throat.

Peng, being Mayor of Peking, is physically and politically near the throne. He has many of the obvious assets of leadership and may one day step into the highest place.

Mao Tse-tung, ruler of a country of more than 3,000,000 square miles with a population near 490,000,000, sits in the centre of this vast web whose meshes reach out to the remotest regions and outposts of China. What manner of man is he?

Shortly after the May Day parade the Indian cultural delegation was invited to meet Mao before attending with him a concert of Chinese music and dance. We waited in the anteroom where, a week before, Chou En-lai had welcomed us to a banquet. It was a rectangular chamber with elaborate carved woodwork and the atmosphere of an Indian durbar. In a shining glass case was a delicately wrought ivory sailing ship.

Mao entered the room with Mrs. Pandit, and his huge, broad frame was magnified by her slight figure. He has a slow bearlike tread and walked with deliberate steps to where we stood and shook each of us by the hand. His palm was soft to the touch, but his grip was firm. He looked you in the eyes as he shook hands, and then stepped back to peer at you again in a measuring way. The famous mole showed in his chin. He exuded blandness and benignity, and gave me the impression of a cross between a Chinese Buddha and Charles Laughton.

Off and on he asked a question or ventured a remark, in a voice thin for a man of his bulk. He said little apart from a few phrases about "peace and Asian friendship."

This farmer's son from Hunan is of the earth, earthy; but he has a guile and subtlety of mind not ordinarily associated with the soil. With a profound knowledge of the Chinese people, particularly of the peasants, he has thought deeply on many problems and reached firm conclusions; and his inner certainty is reflected in an outward calm. His touchstone is experience combined with his own sure instinct.

From the very beginning of the struggle with Chiang Kai-shek, Mao has given the impression of being apart from and yet definitely of the people. A man is a composite bundle of many personalities. In every one of us lurk a Jekyll and a Hyde. Mao's countenance is an interesting mixture of strength and sensuality, of feminine sensitivity and massive masculine sureness and intellect. The plump face with the full lips might belong to a woman. So might the voice. But there is intellect in the vast sweep of forehead and assurance in his carriage and the proud tilt of his head.

There is also ruthlessness. A ruler whose regime has accounted for more than two million lives within three years can entertain no great tenderness for his opponents. Mao's benignity shines only on those who follow him. His wrath strikes all dissenters.

The man is compact of many qualities, some of them unusual and others seen rarely in combination. To a peasant's earthiness he adds a scholar's sensibility. Like Napoleon he is both soldier and administrator; and, though deeply read in Marxism, he is eclectic enough to adapt it to his needs. He is no armchair theorist content to swallow wholesale the gospel according to Marx. Mao is immensely conscious of the fact that in establishing a Communist regime in China he has broken new ground and confounded at least one dogma of Lenin. The Chinese revolution was a peasant, not a proletarian, upheaval. At the same time Mao's realism and pragmatic common sense lead him to flatter Moscow by inflating the role of the proletariat. The hard core of his being is Communist; but he can be resilient, bending himself only in order to break others to his inflexible will.

Mao's combination of qualities makes him a formidable ally— and opponent. Without illusions and without fear, he is also without scruples. That is endemic in the opportunist character of Communism. Others, such as Liu Shao-chi, might interpret the Marxist gospel. Mao expounds it. The *if*'s of history are intriguing, and it is an engaging exercise to speculate what might have been the later course of the Chinese revolution had Mao died, as he very nearly did, on the Long March. With his death the Communist cause would have lost its leaven and yeast. Like Moses, Mao has led his people across the desert wastes to the Promised Land.

He is calculating and audacious. Only an imaginative man could draw as he does, for analogy and illustration, on the treasure house of Chinese tradition and thought. His favourite novel, *Shui Hu Chan* (which Pearl Buck has translated into English under the title *All Men Are Brothers*), details the adventures of a band of robber chieftains and has three major heroes. Does Mao see in them the image of himself, Chu Teh, and Chou En-lai? His gift for improvisation and adaptation has even led him to extract from this novel some useful lessons in tactical and strategic warfare.

Willingness to learn is among his outstanding traits. Gandhi had the majesty of the meek. Mao's imperiousness flows from a mixture of instinctive pride and humility. Deep inside him is a tenderness for the tired earth of China, and the peasant in him clings proudly to the soil. He will always be Chinese. Mao embraced Marxism not merely because it appealed to his sensitivity for the downtrodden and oppressed, but because his practical mind saw in it the answer to China's prayers. The third major trait in his character, ruthlessness, enabled him remorselessly to translate hope into faith and theory into fact.

Many identify Mao's leadership with the beginnings of the Communist party in China. Actually it was not until 1935, some fourteen years after the inaugural session of the National Congress of the Communist party of China was first convened in Shanghai, that Mao was elected chief of the party. He joined it on its foundation in July, 1921, but was reluctant to mortgage his mind wholly to the mentors from Moscow. Cities, said the town-bred masters of the Kremlin, were the "centres of power." Mao disagreed. Power in China, he argued, proceeded from the peasants. Yet significantly even then he was prepared to subdue his minor doubts and hesitations to the major loyalty of Communism. Mao will never be a Tito.

He obeyed the party line when called to order, and even later, while pursuing his own courses, was careful to align them with the broad pattern of Kremlin policy. Ultimately it may be that Chinese Marxism will emerge as Maoism—"the theory," as Liu Shao-chi puts it, "which unites the theories of Marxism-Leninism with the actual practice of the Chinese revolution." The solid theoretical base is Communism as defined by Marx and Engels. But just as Lenin and Stalin claim that their interpretations are more than grafts on the main trunk, so also the Chinese seem to claim today that Maoism is more than a mere accretion on the body basic. It is part of the blood stream and must nourish and enrich the corpus of Communism.

It was not always so. Between 1921 and 1931 the Communist party of China was a house divided against itself. Chen Tu-hsiu, the first Secretary-General of the party, was expelled in August, 1927, for "right opportunism," and is denounced today as a "Trotskyite traitor." He died in 1943, his last days being devoted more to philology than to politics.

Chu Chhu-pai, who succeeded Chen as Secretary-General, regarded Moscow as his spiritual home. He was unquestionably loyal to the Kremlin and died in 1935 before a Kuomintang firing squad. But the volatile Li Li-san was the real power in the four years until he was rebuked and exiled to Moscow in 1931.

In the twilight of the tired twenties Li stood midway between the rural "Chinese faction" represented by Mao and the industrially inclined "Russian faction" led by Chen Shao-yu, better known as Wang Ming. Inevitably he was caught between the two, and after ignominiously beating his breast and confessing the error of his ways, was shipped to Moscow. Not until 1945 did Li return to his country. Today he is Minister of Labour and a member of the central committee of the Communist party.

In 1931 at the first Congress of Soviet representatives at Jui-chin, capital of the Kiangsi Soviet Area, Mao Tse-tung was elected head of the Soviet government. Wang Ming, however, remained the party chief. Not until January, 1935, during a halt on the Long March in Kweichow province, was Mao elected head of the party. He has ruled it since then, and not even the Comintern has dared to interfere. Like Talleyrand, Mao has discovered that nothing succeeds like success.

Closest to him in the Red hierarchy is the gnarled, chunky Chu Teh. Neither Liu Shao-chi nor Chou En-lai is as vital a cog in the governmental machine as the soldier from Szechwan. Chu, born to wealth, has always been a professional soldier, and his loyalty to Mao largely ensures the loyalty of the army, on whose support the regime ultimately depends.

Chu learned the elements of guerrilla warfare as a young battalion commander on the border of Yunnan province not far from Tonkin. This was on the eve of the First World War. He had then a taste for opium and concubines, and as he waxed in military rank—he was a brigadier at thirty-three—his appetite and opulence grew. Following the cynical custom of those warlord days, Chu was prepared to sell his sword to the highest bidder. His trek took him from the wastes of western China to the cities of the coastal belt.

In 1923 he joined the Kuomintang in the service of the Canton regime of Dr. Sun Yat-sen. Something stirred within him. From a soldier of sybaritic habits he suddenly changed to a serious student of military science and politics. In 1924 Chu went to Germany and stayed for a while in Berlin, where he joined the Communist party; later at Göttingen he studied sociology. It is not certain whether he visited Moscow; but he returned to North China by the Trans-Siberian Railway.

Thereafter his association with the Chinese Communist party, if not always open, was close. When early in 1926 Chiang Kai-shek seized Canton and then turned on Shanghai, Chu went temporarily underground. He set about organising an army and a base. In the mountainous terrain of Hunan and Kiangsi he built up the nucleus of the Red army. He was careful to rely on popular support and nursed the good will of the peasants. For six years, from 1928 to 1934, Chu operated with his guerrillas. In that year he joined forces with Mao, who brought along a ragged band of rebels. The meeting took place on Chingkangshan, a mountain peak in southern Kiangsi.

From then onwards the two men worked as one, merging their identities so closely that to the outer world the Chu-Mao army was long believed to be commanded by one man. This basic bond survives. Chu is as complementary and vital to Mao today as he was in the days when they trekked from Kiangsi to Shensi and moved finally across the Yellow River to rout the armies of Chiang Kai-shek.

Chu's grip on the army is firm, operating through three trusted lieutenants—the youthful Lin Piao, Moscow-trained Liu Po-cheng, and the politically conscious Peng Teh-huai. These three generals administer three vital areas, Southwest China, the North-west, and Central South-China.

The contrast between Chiang's soldiery, whom I saw eight years ago in Chungking, and Mao's Red army was striking. "You do not use good iron to make nails," they said in Kuomintang China. "You do not use good men to make soldiers." There was something pathetic in the wan, forlorn look of Chiang's soldiers, many of them incredibly young, ill equipped, in shoddy grey uniforms and grass sandals.

The soldiers I saw in Mao's China, particularly Mukden, were altogether different. They strode the earth in adequate attire and with an air. Theirs was the kingdom and the glory. They were not drawn entirely from the peasantry: schools and colleges have responded generously to the government's recruiting drives. In Shanghai a European missionary remarked on the new sense of patriotism evident among the educated young.

"Many thousands of students," he remarked, "have volunteered in the last recruitment drive. It was unusual, in fact unprecedented. In my own middle school, although over a hundred volunteered, only about forty cadets were chosen. This shows that the Communists have sufficient man power at their disposal to be selective."

China's strength from time immemorial has hinged on two facts: the extent of her territory and the number of her people. Today, with an army of some six million, she is drawing on the latter. The time may come to exploit the former. It will not be the first occasion when she has traded space for time.

Liu Shao-chi provides another type of powder and shot. He is the ideological quartermaster-general, doling out Marxist provender as and when the occasion requires. Some say he is nearer Moscow than Mao. I doubt it. He has a habit, physically and politically, of merging with his immediate background, and there is no doubt that he speaks in the accents of Moscow even while he uses the language of Peking. But who knows what impulse moves him? Some describe him as "the second most important man in Red China." Because Mao can sustain himself so long as his regime lasts inside China, and because his own people would more readily listen to Peking than to Moscow, it is open to question whether Liu rates above Chu. Mao has enough military sustenance to need no ideological ballast. His is the word. From Caesar one may appeal only to Caesar.

Liu, it is said, has no existence apart from the party. At the concert after our interview with Mao, I sat two rows in front of Liu and his handsome wife, who were only a row in front of Mao. Chinese etiquette requires that in a theatre the guests be seated in front of the host.

Mao smoked incessantly throughout the concert, and though he responded visibly to the verbal bouquets showered on him from the stage his manner suggested that these were not unusual. Liu sat impassively through the performance. He has the mien not merely of an acolyte but of an anchorite, and even the proximity of his attractive wife did not lessen the impression of a faint fragrance of incense and myrrh.

Like Mao he comes from Hunan, though physically and temperamentally the two men seem poles apart. Liu is slim and ascetic. Mao has the broad bulk and the look of one who has savoured life fully: he exudes good and glad living. Liu is intrinsically an introvert accustomed to expressing problems in the high, stilted idiom of Marxist thought and writing. Mao seems to be an exuberant extrovert content to state the same problem in the homely, earthy idiom of his own people. He is much nearer to them than Liu, who, although he once worked as a miner in the Wu-Han cities which constitute the industrial heart of China (Hankow, Hanyang, and Wuchang), moves in a remote ideological stratosphere. He is little known outside China except, of course, in Moscow. But significantly he was reported to be at the Kremlin in 1952 shortly after the official Chinese delegation headed by Chou En-lai had left the Russian capital. Liu was present at the last official obsequies of the Cominform.

His is probably a bilateral function. If he is adept at explaining the New China to Moscow he is probably equally glib in interpreting the Kremlin's mind to Peking. Liu functions as Mao's ideological life line to Peking and simultaneously as Russia's pipe line to China.

What of Chou En-lai? Although widely known abroad he impresses me as having far less influence inside China than people of other nations think. Chou, who comes from Kiangsi, spent his youth in Manchuria. He is the most Westernised Communist in the upper hierarchy of the government. Chu Teh and Li Li-san were his contemporaries in Europe. But while they remain intrinsically and outwardly Chinese, Chou has more than a slight veneer of the West. He is spruce, startlingly handsome, and there is spring in his step. His carriage and manners, even the alert look in the deep brown eyes, bespeak an Occidental rather than an Oriental influence. Withal, Chou is a shrewd, watchful, wary man. Though seemingly frank he will give nothing away.

He has reason to be more cautious than most, for although he has been a Communist from youth his Marxism proceeds more from emotional idealism than from profound study. Chiang Kai-shek, mindful perhaps of the Sian incident of 1936 when Chou saved his life, liked to refer to him as "a reasonable Communist." Chou has felt more than thought his way to Communism. Within the party he is regarded as an intellectual lightweight. He has flair and a certain flamboyance, but his Marxism seems meretricious. Yet it is interesting to recall that for a time after his return to China in 1924 his influence rated higher than Mao's.

Even today Mao treats him largely as his oracle on foreign policy. There is reason and indeed some evidence to believe that in Li Li-san's struggle with the central committee Chou inclined towards Li. But he accommodated himself quickly to the new situation which arose with Li's ostracism and exile. The same adaptability makes him a misleading adviser. He seems to be more interested today in providing the premises for Mao's conclusions than in reaching conclusions of his own. And in the foreign field Mao walks uncertainly.

China's ruler knows his country and people, but it is doubtful whether he understands the world outside them. Mao was never away from his country until December, 1949, when he visited Russia. Although he went through the conventional Communist motions and made the appropriate statements and speeches, there was nothing of the starry-eyed idolater about him. Pictures taken during his stay inside the Soviet tabernacle show him as no worshipper. He stands aloof and proudly, even a little disdainfully on his own pinnacle.

In Mao's reckoning, Chou is perhaps a useful foil to Liu Shao-chi, who leans strongly towards Moscow. Chou, like Mao, is basically pro-Chinese, though the present international balance leaves Peking with no alternative but to genuflect before the Kremlin. A day may come when China, equating her strength with the Soviet, will refuse to bow the knee to the Russian Baal and assert, even as she claims today, an equal status with the Soviet.

6

HAMMER AND SICKLE

I saw my first Russians at the May Day parade in Peking. Flanking the Indian delegation to the right were members of the Russian Embassy headed by the Ambassador. On the other side of the Soviet bloc were the Koreans, dressed for the most part in Western costume and looking vaguely enigmatic and uneasy. The Burmese in their fluttering headdresses stood behind us. They chattered gaily.

As the Soviet Ambassador strode forward to shake hands with Mrs. Pandit the medals on both sides of his chest clanked noisily. His entourage were almost equally decorative. "Not Solomon in all his glory was arrayed as one of these," murmured an irreverent colleague.

The Russians certainly stood out in the drab assembly of foreign diplomats and visitors who crowded the stands. Even the brave black Homburgs of the British Negotiating Mission, rising sombrely in the background, seemed weighed—and worn—with sad discretion.

"If Indo-China were to fall to Ho Chi-minh," remarked a foreign diplomat some days later, "it would be difficult to assess the extent of Chinese influence in that country. It's the same with regard to Russian influence in China."

Ostensibly there is small evidence of this influence. The Russians we saw were few and far between though the Chinese readily admitted their dependence on Russia for a certain amount of technical advice and aid. The Hwai River project, which is one of the Red regime's show pieces, has a Russian technical adviser who figured prominently in a painting displayed to visitors. Some of the machinery and capital equipment of Manchurian factories is of Soviet make. In a factory at Mukden the only two high-precision lathes we saw were of Russian manufacture. Russian books, magazines, and pamphlets abound in bookstores, and quite a number of students to whom I spoke at various academic centres were studying Russian as a second language.

Soviet influence grows perceptibly as one travels north. In southern and central China the picture of Mao is invariably flanked in public institutes by those of Marx, Engels, Lenin, and Stalin; but in Manchuria, particularly in Mukden, Mao's portrait stands alone with Stalin. The signboards inside our hotel at Mukden and in the local theatres were in Chinese and Russian. In a railway waiting room in Manchuria, I came across a Russian newspaper file. Here also busts of Stalin and Mao stared bleakly from the mantelpiece.

One evening we engaged our interpreters in a discussion. For some days they had been probing us gently in an effort to discover our reactions to their country. We thought the moment propitious to probe them.

"You regard India as semicolonial," one of us remarked. "You think we are still under the British influence. Well, we think you are greatly under the influence of the Russians."

The reaction was strong and immediate.

"We've never concealed our dependence on Russia for advice in some fields," said one of them. "But have you ever seen a Russian order a Chinese about?"

We had not, and externally the behaviour of such Russians as

we saw in the streets and hotels was correct. Even the Russian
advisers are careful to transmit their orders through Chinese intermediaries. There was no visible sign of overlordship, and in fact
the Chinese dislike for "foreign devils" extends, a veteran European resident assured me, to Russians and even to fellow Asians.
That may well be, for the Chinese tradition of aloofness is almost
as old as time. With other foreigners the Russians are surrepti-
tiously referred to as "long noses."

I thought the interpreter's emphasis on external evidence characteristic. Because a Russian dare not order a Chinese about in
public there could, in his reasoning, be no political overlordship.
Imperialism, in Chinese as in most Eastern minds, is identified
with certain external manifestations to which the West has
inured them. It is equated with gunboats and marines, with the
cuffing of "coolies," colour bar, rape, the bayonet, and the gun.
Absence of these in a foreigner implies a friend, not a foe.

All around him today the Chinese sees his own countrymen in
the seats of power. Authority may speak to him through various
persons—through officials, soldiers, policemen, *kanpu*, and com-
missars; but they are Chinese persons and Chinese voices. For the
most part the Russians we saw were concentrated in the cities;
and more than four-fifths of the Chinese reside on the land.
Probably fewer than twenty Chinese in every thousand have seen
Russians.

Yet just as a sense of power flows pervasively from China's
chosen few to the multitudinous masses, so also the Soviet influence pervading Peking seeps imperceptibly to the Chinese
people. The May Day parade provided a striking illustration. On
Tuesday April 29, 1952, the *Shanghai News* printed on its front
page the May Day calls issued by the Communist party of the
Soviet Union. On the 30th, the eve of May Day, the front page
of that newspaper contained the May Day calls of the National
Committee of the Chinese People's Political Consultative Conference. A comparison between the two sets of calls revealed
some illuminating features.

There were 58 Chinese May Day calls compared with 59

Russian. The first call of the former echoed the first of the latter. "Long live May Day—the day of international solidarity of the working people, the day of fraternity of workers of all countries!" ran the Russian. "Long live May Day—day of solidarity of the working people of the world!" cried the Chinese.

Call 4 of the Russians sent "fraternal greetings to the great Chinese people who have attained new successes in building the people's democratic China." Call 9 of the Chinese reciprocated the compliment: "Salute the great Soviet people who are engaged in construction works of Communism! Long live the unbreakable friendship between China and the Soviet Union!"

Both sets of calls honoured the Korean people. The Chinese termed them "heroic" while the Russian dubbed them "courageous." Both sent greetings to "the Japanese people who are vigorously fighting for national liberation." Aside from this, the Russian invocations referred largely to European countries such as Germany and Yugoslavia. Viet Nam and Formosa figured prominently in the Chinese list, which joined with the Russian in characterising Western Germany as "a base of imperialist aggression in Europe."

Two items in the Chinese litany were of particular interest and significance, for both betrayed the font and source of Peking's inspiration. Call 21 on the Chinese rota exhorted: "Long live the world camp of peace and democracy *headed by the Soviet Union.*" The Russian list nowhere mentioned Mao. But the Chinese hymn of hate and love rose to a shrill crescendo in Call 58: "Long live Generalissimo Stalin, great leader of the working people of the world!"

Clearly here were clues as to who led and who followed. Russia paid the piper and called the tune. Perhaps too much might be read into these organised chants; but slogans constitute vital weapons in the Communist armoury, and their pattern on this occasion was revealing.

Mao's primary loyalty is to Marx more than to Moscow. But just as earlier he ignored Moscow's directive and built his revolution on the peasantry rather than on the proletariat, so now he senses that conditions, internal and external, demand a closer association with the Kremlin, ideologically and on the international plane. He soft-pedals Russia's denudation of the Manchurian factories while simultaneously he inflates Moscow's role in the Chinese revolution. If he follows a different course from the Russian in land reform it is because he still believes in adapting means while inflexibly preserving ends. The end here is collectivisation.

Even his concept of the New Democracy, with its recognition of a place for the private capitalist and petty trader, is not so original as many outside observers believe. Over thirty years ago Lenin wrote that the Communists "must enter into a temporary alliance with bourgeois democracy in colonial and backward countries, but must not merge with it, and must unconditionally preserve the independence of the proletarian movement even in its most rudimentary form." That is precisely what Mao is doing. By this "temporary alliance" the Chinese Communists have been enabled to set up the solid fabric of their government with no great dislocation to themselves or the country. It has also protected the economic structure from undue stress and strain.

Fear of the emergence of a new bourgeoisie on the proletarian front goes hand in hand with fear of the growth of a new landlord class in the agrarian field. Both fears have recently provoked strong reactions. The San Fan and Wu Fan movements were a manifestation of the first, while Kao Kang's increasingly belligerent warnings against "the narrow-mindedness of the peasants who think in terms of increasing production only in order to enrich their families" are an expression of the second.

Except, therefore, in spearheading his revolution with the peasantry, Mao has not deviated to any great extent from the precepts of Moscow. And even here he now seeks to conform. Where his practice has differed elsewhere from the Moscow model it has accorded with the precepts of the Kremlin.

Mao, being a loyal Marxist, can never be anti-Moscow though

the day may come when he will equate China with Russia. As Liu Shao-chi emphasises, Maoism "unites the theories of Marxism-Leninism with the actual practice of the Chinese revolution." The success of this revolution is of immense significance in Moscow's eyes, particularly in relation to the countries of Asia; but, as certain Soviet spokesmen have not been slow to point out, it would be risky to regard the Chinese experience as a stereotype or blueprint for a "people's democratic revolution" in other Asian countries. These might not be able to produce a revolutionary army such as Communist China threw up.

Today China is content to move a step behind Russia. Peking regards Moscow as representing a more advanced stage of Socialism than its own. And because of this Mao believes that the things which apply to the Russians need not apply to the Chinese. The two countries present the picture of one colossus marching behind the other. But both march in step.

Not only does China look to Russia for ideological sustenance, but she relies on her for material aid. The blockade of the Western powers leaves her in any case with no alternative. China would have liked to trade with Japan, and until the outbreak of the Korean War in June, 1950, she seemed to be willing to deal with Western commercial interests and business houses inside the country. In fact the Communist regime's early concentration on controlling its currency and improving its communications led many European businessmen to believe that trade prospects were encouraging. As government monopolies expanded, the sphere of private trade was bound to shrink. Even so, many foreigners, particularly the British, were hopeful that China would still be a market for imported goods and a source of raw materials.

If these hopes have been disappointed the fault is not entirely China's. Peking's seizure of United States property in China only followed Washington's freezing of the Red regime's assets in America, and it is doubtful if Peking was the greater sufferer of the two in this transaction. With the intensification of the blockade China endeavoured to increase her commerce with Russia and with the satellite countries of Poland, Czechoslovakia, and East Germany. Action begot reaction. China, albeit desirous of finding natural outlets for her trade, was driven deeper into the economic maw of the Soviet.

Belief that the blockade will ultimately produce political repercussions against Russia is a dangerous delusion. The effect is precisely the opposite. Gratitude for economic favours received must strengthen, not weaken, the political ties which hold Moscow and Peking together. Nor is China's economic structure liable to be dented badly by these brittle and boomerang tactics. A predominantly agricultural country is more resilient against a trade embargo than a heavily industrialised State.

"Without foreign aid," remarked Shanghai's Mayor, General Chen Yi, "our industrial regeneration will take longer—but it will come. Why should Asia not pool her economic resources and lean less heavily on the West?"

To China the West signifies not only economic blockade but the growing threat of a military and political stranglehold. In Western calculations Formosa might be a vital link in the defensive chain stretching from the Aleutians to the Philippines. China sees this island as a potential springboard for an attack on her mainland.

"After all," observed a mild-looking professor at Peking, "Taiwan [Formosa] is less than a hundred miles from the coast of Fukien. It is nearly 5,000 miles from America's western seaboard. Who is the aggressor, and who the aggressed?"

In Chinese eyes the arc of fortifications extending from Tokyo to Korea through Okinawa and Formosa to the Philippines and Hong Kong constitutes the mailed fist of the West. Confronted with it, Peking turns its gaze more intently on Moscow.

Even in the absence of these pressure tactics China would have found a place in the Soviet camp. "Internationally," according to a statement by Mao in July, 1949, "we belong to the anti-imperialist front headed by the U.S.S.R., and we can look only for genuine friendly aid from that front." On this issue China's leader has steadfastly refused to take the middle road. "To sit on the fence is impossible."

Yet in 1949 Mao was willing to "do business" with the West both economically and politically. Both internally and externally China had calculated on an interim period before complete identity with the Soviet was achieved. Had America's policy of building a *cordon sanitaire* around Red China dislocated that country's internal economy and made closer approximation with Russia difficult, it would have served a purpose. But its only effect has been to heighten the tempo of China's internal efforts to achieve full socialism while strengthening Peking's communion with Moscow on the international plane.

"If only America had retained some links with China," sighed a European diplomat, "the position of foreign missionaries and businessmen in this country would have been better. As it is, the mere fact that I inquire from time to time about those interned or detained serves as a small deterrent. The government knows that the fate of these people is being watched—and will be reported."

The Sino-Soviet alliance appears to be popular in China, but it has not always been so. A frontier longer than any other in the world stretches between the two countries, and proximity has nourished age-long fears and suspicions. For years Moscow's eyes have been focussed on three enormous areas of North China: Manchuria, Sinkiang, and Outer Mongolia.

From Alma Ata in Russian Turkestan to Sinkiang is a distance of 700 air-miles, and until the advent of the Communist regime Peking's only access to this region was across the Gobi Desert which took six weeks to traverse by caravan. Sinkiang now forms part of China's Northwest area.

Outer Mongolia, long regarded as Chinese territory, was absorbed into the Russian orbit in the early twenties, and the Sino-Soviet Treaty of 1945 between the Kuomintang government and Moscow affirmed its independence. A year later Outer Mongolia applied unsuccessfully for membership in the United Nations.

Manchuria has proved to be a more intractable problem. The Chinese Eastern Railway linking Siberia to Vladivostok and running from Harbin through Dairen to Port Arthur was once Soviet-controlled. Through it Russia straddled Manchuria. By a cynical bargain contracted behind China's back at Yalta in February, 1945, Moscow was allowed to recover these valuable possessions as the price of her entry into the war against Japan.

The Sino-Soviet Treaty of 1945 declared Dairen a free port and allowed Russia the use of Port Arthur as a naval base. It placed the major Manchurian railways—there are four other lines than the Chinese Eastern—under joint Sino-Soviet control. These railways are now known collectively as the Chinese Changchun Railway.

Since the proclamation of the People's Republic of China in October, 1949, Peking has made two pilgrimages to Moscow. On Mao's visit in the winter of 1949–1950 a new Sino-Soviet Treaty was signed February 14, 1950. This abrogated the Treaty of 1945, and Mao returned to Peking with Russian promises that the Soviet's half-share in the Chinese Changchun Railway would be surrendered on the conclusion of a treaty with Japan or not later than the end of 1952. Russia also agreed to relinquish Port Arthur with the same proviso. Although Peking was allowed to administer Dairen its future was left for further determination on the conclusion of a peace treaty with Japan. Reports were current during our visit to China that a Russian garrison was still stationed at this port. The prescribed time limits are interesting, for they suggest that Stalin was anxious to put Mao on probation for a period before parting with sanctions held.

In August, 1952, Chou En-lai's visit to Moscow set in spate another train of speculation. Accompanying him to the Russian capital were Chen Yu, Deputy Prime Minister, who is also China's chief economic planner; General Su Yu, deputy chief of staff; and Li Fu-chun, chairman of the committee of economic and financial affairs. The official communiqué announcing the outcome of the talks was markedly reticent. It revealed little beyond announcing the return of the Chinese Changchun Railway to Peking and the retention by Russia of the naval base at Port Arthur. Dairen did not figure in the announcement, nor was there any mention of economic aid beyond the $300,000,000 of credits which the 1950 Treaty granted China. The probationary period continues.

Between the two treaties Peking had become involved in the Korean War. New portents loomed on the horizon. Among these were the threat of a militarist Japan, the signing of the San Francisco Treaty, Tokyo's defence pact with Washington, and the building up of America's military ring in the Pacific. Almost certainly a Soviet aid programme of more ambitious proportions figured on the agenda. Apart from financial help Peking counts on a larger flow of military equipment from its ally. It is doubtful whether Chinese arsenals can turn out more than small arms and artillery. For aircraft, tanks, and modern naval craft Peking is dependent on Moscow. While arming China, Russia is unlikely to hasten her development into a military equal. It is noticeable that Moscow's industrial help in the shape of capital goods lags far behind her supplies of finished war material.

Sino-Soviet relations are viewed more clearly in this altered context. Between 1950 and 1952 the entire Chinese prospective, internal and external, has seen some radical shifts. Early in 1950 many groups of Chinese looked with disfavour on the close alignment with Moscow, recalling resentfully that Russia behind China's back had exploited the war situation to restore the *status quo ante bellum* in Manchuria. Hundreds of millions of dollars' worth of plant and material were removed by Russia from Manchuria on the plea that it was war booty. Even the fact that the Red regime initially condoned the Sino-Soviet Treaty of 1945 did not prevent public opinion from criticising it as "unequal." As late as May, 1950, the pro-Peking *Ta Kung Pao* of Hong Kong was elaborately explaining the reasons for the revised treaty of February, 1950; and it is significant that this arrangement provided for returning "gratis to the government of the People's

Republic of China the property acquired by Soviet economic organisations from Japanese owners in Manchuria." Inside China, newspapers such as the *Progressive Daily* in April, 1949, characterised as "evil slander and shameless propaganda" accusations that the U.S.S.R. was imperialistic.

The Russian retention of Port Arthur, which dominates the approaches to Tientsin and Peking, came in for particular criticism. Yet in 1952 its continued retention raised no perceptible murmur. The Korean War, with the tightening of the West's defensive ring around China, has undoubtedly drawn Peking and Moscow together. With a closer community of interests in the Far East, Russia's continuance in Port Arthur was accepted as both logical and sensible. Even the return of the Chinese Changchun Railway was recognised as liable to be hedged by an understanding designed to allow Moscow full use of this vital highway in a crisis.

Peking has been drawn deeper into the Soviet orbit. No ideological differences separate China from Russia, and during the past three years China's growing economic and military dependence on her ally has strengthened the bonds. From the periphery of Soviet influence the sheer weight of events is pulling China to the gravitational centre. A global war will throw her into the waiting arms of Moscow.

"People," warned Chou En-lai in 1949, "will be disappointed if they think there will ever be a Tito in China." This was not mere wishful thinking nor whistling to keep the courage up. A year earlier Liu Shao-chi in his book *Internationalism and Nationalism* had emphatically endorsed the Cominform's condemnation of Titoism as "bourgeois nationalism." Liu recalled Mao's warning in his *New Democracy* that the choice is between uniting with the Soviet Union and uniting with imperialism. "It must be one or the other. That is the line of demarcation between patriotism and betrayal of one's own country, between revolution and counter-revolution, between progress and retrogression for any nation. Opposing the Soviet Union will surely be serving the interest of imperialism and betraying the interest of one's own nation."

The West cannot say it has not been warned. China may take no directives from Russia, but she is subject to Soviet influence. In so far as their enemies are the same and their victims identical, the two countries lean for support on each other. If Mao cannot do without Moscow, neither can Moscow easily disown Mao. Each needs the other, and Peking seems to be willing to play the junior partner until it can speak as an equal. Although it was distasteful to national pride, China's Red regime affirmed the independent status of Outer Mongolia during the 1950 negotiations, thereby setting its seal on the Kuomintang government's recognition of the same fact in 1945.

Has there been a tacit share-out in the two partners' spheres of influence, with China claiming a preponderating voice in Asia? Recent developments suggest that Mao, albeit cautiously, is staking his claim to a major role in the Orient, thereby seeking to equate China's position in the East with Russia's role in Europe. Moscow's reluctance to concede this position is also evident.

Significantly, the holding of the international peace conference at Peking in October, 1952, excited no great enthusiasm in the Kremlin. Russia does not relish the spectacle of China stealing her pacifist thunder and posing as the high pontiff of world peace. The tone of the Soviet press was peevish and impatient. Peking's prime objective at this assembly was to demonstrate its leadership of the Communist bloc in the East. The much advertised pledge of the Indian and Pakistani delegations to achieve a solution on Kashmir was one manifestation of this resolve. Another was provided by the open letter addressed to the Japanese people by Dr. Kuo Mo-jo, chairman of the Chinese Peace Committee. In this carefully calculated epistle, which was released before the conference, Dr. Kuo Mo-jo promised that Japan would have a prominent place on the agenda.

Russian reluctance to regard the Chinese revolution as a blueprint for colonial countries in Asia is interestingly revealed by a discussion of the character of the people's democracy in the Orient which was held at the Oriental Studies Institute of the U.S.S.R. Academy of Sciences in November, 1951.*

Opening the discussion, M. Zhukov, corresponding member of the Academy, observed that the Chinese People's Republic had succeeded in creating a united people's democratic front and this was of immense significance. "Traces of its fruitful influence," he remarked, "can easily be found in the documents of the Communist Party of India and the Workers' Party of Viet Nam." At the same time he warned that it would be risky to regard the Chinese experience as "some kind of stereotype" for people's democratic revolutions in other Asian countries. "The masses of the peoples of the Orient," said Comrade Zhukov, "who have already embarked on the path of people's democracy for national liberation and for peace harbour the greatest trust and love for the Soviet Union and Comrade Stalin."

Sixteen persons took part in the discussion which followed. Most of them stressed the "special role" of the Chinese revolution "in the forming of the programme of struggle for a people's democracy" particularly in India and the countries of Southeast Asia. One speaker, G. I. Levinson, referred to the substantial Chinese populations—45 per cent in Malaya and 20 per cent in Thailand—which maintained close political ties with China; "and this," he said, "promotes the assimilation by the countries of Southeast Asia of the experience of the Chinese revolution which is being intensively studied and spread by the Communist parties of these countries."

Following these effusive tributes came verbal dampers from Comrades Balbushevich and Nasenko, described as "specialists on India," and from M. Zhukov, who summed up the discussion. It was risky, said the two comrades, to view the Chinese revolution and its development as an obligatory model for other Asian

* The full text of the proceedings appears in the *Journal of the U.S.S.R. Academy of Sciences*, History and Philosophy Series, Vol. IX, No. 1, Jan.-Feb. (published in May), 1952, pp. 80–87.

countries. They referred to India, "where we have seen the full error of mechanically applying the experience of the Chinese revolution," and went on to say that "the transformation in China from the people's democratic revolution to a socialist revolution will be reflected not so much in a change in the composition of the regime but chiefly in a change in the programme of the regime, in a change of its policy, in the fact that the proletariat will turn to its proletarian task—the building up of a socialist society." M. Zhukov in summing up the discussion pointed out that, while it would be absurd to belittle the Chinese experience, it must at the same time "not be made a fetish applicable to all situations in Asian countries." Obviously Moscow does not have so rosy a view of Mao's revolution as Peking would perhaps desire.

There seems to be little doubt that Mao regards Asia as his particular sphere of influence. Like Stalin he is a realist. Dependent as he now is on Soviet help, he is unlikely to do anything to offend or even embarrass Moscow. But vis-à-vis the Kremlin he still stands much on his dignity. If he relies on Russia for economic and military aid he is conscious of the fact—and is careful to make Moscow aware of it—that China does the fighting. For the moment Russia has the better of the bargain. But Mao knows how to bide his time. There will be no crisis in Sino-Soviet relations so long as the present emergency exists. But should the Russian and Chinese rulers survive the crisis to find Europe and Asia at their feet, as they scheme and hope, Communism will have reached another crucial turning point in its history. Then the Man of Peking will confront the Man of Moscow, and both must decide whether like a bourgeois coin Communism can continue as one piece with two faces.

7

DOWN THE HWAI RIVER

The Hwai River throbbed with movement and life. Crowds lined the waterfront at Pengpu as the motorboat drawing our two barges, which were lashed together, nosed its way up the river. The afternoon sun glinted on the sails of scores of small craft crowding the port. As we moved into the open river the green fields rolled away into the distance. We passed villages and tiny hamlets. Off and on, a junk with huge, rectangular sails swept by. These sails were red or white or black and often tattered, giving the junks a rakish, piratical look. Whole families lived aboard. There were fisherfolk in blue jeans, the women dressed in black, and children gay in red waved a greeting while infants toddled uncertainly, tethered by a leading string to a bar or post.

We had come to Pengpu across the rolling corn fields of Shantung after a visit to Kü-fow, where Confucius was buried. Eyeing our bourgeois "softness," the Chinese seemed sceptical of our ability to endure the rigours of the Hwai River journey. The women of the party, they argued, should in any case be dissuaded from coming. And since illness had taken toll of some of our older members it would be wiser for them to stay behind. Actually the four days' journey in the barges was no great ordeal. Accommodation aboard was perhaps a little cramped, and sanitation was a highly basic business. Quite half of our party of fourteen had dropped out either voluntarily or under a last-minute show of authority and *force majeure*. Mrs. Pandit insisted on coming, and so did Durgabai, the always cheerful, resourceful woman lawyer who is now a member of India's Planning Commission. These two and Lili Gazdar, Mrs. Pandit's versatile secretary, were the only women in our party.

There was, however, another woman aboard. She was Chien Chen-ying, by profession a hydraulic engineer and deputy chief of the engineering department of the Hwai River Harnessing Committee.

Chien was a remarkable woman. Of all the women I met or saw in China, none impressed me more than this ambling, awkward Donald Duck of a woman whose intelligence, fervour, and spirit gave her personality a luminous quality quite out of keeping with her appearance. Throughout the four days on the river Chien was clad in the regulation blue uniform with an open-neck dark green shirt. She waddled rather than walked. Her thin arms jerked like a marionette's. Her gestures were clumsy. But on her face was the dedicated look of a saint or martyr rapt in her cause. She was, of course, an ardent Communist, and though educated at Shanghai and therefore, I suspect, conversant with English she never once spoke to us except through an interpreter. Underlying her manner and speech was a note of disdain.

Even before we embarked on this river journey we knew something of China's vast waterways. In India the monsoon season sees the peasants scanning the skies. The gaze of China's peasants also sweeps the skies, but as often it scans the horizon where swollen rivers and broken dykes mean ruination for millions. China is dominated by three great waterways—the Hwang Ho, or Yellow River, the Yangtze, and the West, or Pearl, River. They drain respectively North, Central, and South China. Curving through the three provinces of Honan, Anhwei, and Kiangsu is the 600-mile-long Hwai River, which drains an area of some 86,000 square miles and has more than two hundred tributaries. This area of Middle China lies between the Yellow and Yangtze rivers and grows both the wheat of the north and the rice of the south.

In few countries does nature take a heavier toll than in China, where the Yellow River is traditionally known as "China's Sorrow." Between the twenty-third century B.C. and 1938 this waterway has changed its course through the provinces of Hopeh, Shantung, and Kiangsu seven times, flooding many thousands of square miles of land and causing vast damage to life and property. In June, 1938, during a severe engagement between Chiang Kaishek's troops and the Japanese in central Honan the river dykes at Chungmow, according to the Kuomintang, gave way under fire. According to the Communists, Chiang deliberately destroyed the dykes in order to divert the waters southward in the path of the invaders, quite indifferent to the suffering he thereby caused to his own people.

Whatever the reason, the dykes undoubtedly gave way, and the waters of the Hwang Ho, following the Chialu and Tashu rivers, entered the Hwai River and spilled finally into the East China Sea off northern Kiangsu. Half a million people were killed; the damage caused was extensive, and the drainage system of the Hwai River was paralysed.

Little was done to restore the damage until the Communists assumed power in 1949. "Nine years out of ten the crops failed." That at least is the peasants' verdict on the Kuomintang regime. The Hwai River valley has always been notorious for its droughts and floods. In the six hundred and fifty years from the fourteenth to the twentieth century local tradition speaks of 935 such visitations.

In 1950 Mao declared that "the Hwai River project must be harnessed." Of China's multi-purpose projects this undertaking is the largest. It aims to end the floods by controlling the river waters; to regulate the river by dykes and dredging; to conserve water for irrigation purposes; to develop 1,250 miles of navigable highways; and to build power stations. When completed in 1955 (the present expectation) the project will free about thirty million acres of land from floods and will irrigate about eight million acres containing some seventeen million people. The total power generated will be 13,750 kilowatts.

"All this," observed Chien Chen-ying, "may not seem a great engineering feat. We do not say it is. What I want you to remember is that the project is built entirely with Chinese material and with Chinese hands."

Man power is China's greatest asset, and the manner in which her rulers are utilising it to offset deficiencies in machinery and technical equipment offers an interesting study. "Numbers," said Napoleon, "annihilate." They also create. The Hwai River project, as Chien confessed, is no great feat of engineering by Western standards; but it is impressive as an example of what man power can achieve with no great aid of machinery.

The countryside was low-lying, and as we approached our destination, the Lung Ho-chi dam, which controls the middle valley of the river, we saw vast tracts of land submerged although the rains were still two months away. In the middle stream were eight lakes, large and small, with a storage capacity of 7,600,-000,000 cubic yards of water. There were dykes along the perimeters.

"Formerly," said Chien, "the peak flowing rate here was 17,000 cubic yards per second. We have reduced it to 8,500 cubic yards."

The day before we reached the Lung Ho-chi dam, Chien explained the project in detail with the help of maps and charts. She knew the answer to every question and never once faltered in a five-hour discussion between lunch and dinner. She was cool, clear-headed, and concise.

Work on this project began in November, 1950, and the first stage was completed by July, 1951. In this period one reservoir and four storage lakes were completed, while the renovated dykes controlled 820 square miles of land. Some 550 miles of the river course were dredged. Within eighty days 29,000,000 cubic yards of earth were dug up by 270,000 rural workers, and 116 culverts and sluices were completed. These were the figures as Chien retailed them.

Whether they represent the truth or approximate closely to it is anybody's guess. I have no reason to disbelieve them, for those members of the Indian Embassy who had earlier visited the project generally confirmed Chien's picture. Such facts and figures can only be tested with detailed data or visual proof. But it would be unfair to infer from this that the Chinese were "shooting a line," or that we automatically accepted every detail as unimpeachable.

Our visit coincided with the second year of the project. In this period it was hoped to construct three more storage reservoirs including a large dam at Fu So Ling. Irrigation canals covering 100 miles were projected. In the winter of 1951 some 500,000 rural workers were engaged, and in the summer of 1952 as many as 800,000. These dug up 209,000,000 cubic yards of earthwork. It was claimed that twenty-two sluices were constructed and at one time more than two million rural workers toiled on the project.

Actually, on reaching the constructed Lung Ho-chi dam we saw few workers. The explanation was that, the dam being completed, the workers had moved away. We were shown huge photographs of workers swarming over the banks of the river and busily engaged in rearing various structures.

"Here," said Chien, "there is only a skeleton staff. But farther down the river thousands of villagers and peasants are on the job."

We went no farther and therefore had no opportunity of seeing them. There is no doubt, however, that the Chinese government has succeeded in mobilising well over two million rural workers on the job. Foreign observers confirmed this.

Does forced labour enter into the mass recruitment? It is difficult to say. Our prolonged grilling of Chien Chen-ying yielded some interesting facts. According to her, the peasants working on the project came only from the three provinces of Honan, Kiangsu, and Anhwei which the Hwai River traverses. They generally work between the autumn and spring harvests, when they are idle on the land. Most of their labour is concentrated on putting up the earthworks, and on an average they provide eighty working days per year. They are voluntary workers and receive accommodation, a travelling allowance, and free medical aid. They are also compensated for any loss in time due to rains. Their minimum wage is the money equivalent of four catties of rice per day. Payment is on a piece-rate basis and for output above the average an additional incentive bonus is paid. Most of these peasants spend the money equivalent of 3½ catties of rice per day.

There are also peasants who work throughout the year. They are paid in accordance with the ruling rate in the village areas where they normally work, and some earn as much as the money equivalent of eight to ten catties of rice per day. But this, of course, is not the average rate.

We were curious to know how the agrarian land reforms were made applicable to these peasants.

Chien explained. "They generally benefit by the change," she remarked. "They are compensated while at work both for the accommodation and land they would have enjoyed under the agrarian reforms. And when they complete their chores they are generally resettled on better land."

Aside from the two million rural workers there are thousands of technical workers, mainly masons and mechanics, labouring on the project. Besides skilled workers they number some 16,000. They are drawn from cities and towns and are paid according to the rate they earned at their previous employment. They also receive travelling expenses and are compensated for any necessary additional expenditure. Some peasants become skilled workers and are then paid according to this category.

Nearly six hundred civil and hydraulic engineering students and professors work on the project. In 1950 they were drawn from the third-year students in the universities of East China. In 1951 it was the turn of the Central and West China universities. In all, students and professors from eighteen universities have helped in departments as varied as geology, hydraulics, engineering, surveying, and field work. Students are paid their living expenses plus transportation charges. Their studies are not interrupted, because by a government decree the one year's practical work they put in at the project exempts them from the additional one year's practical experience which students are ordinarily required to complete at the end of their course. Professors are paid the salaries they earn, with additional allowances for field work plus transportation expenses.

The miracle of the Hwai River valley project lies in the vast mobilisation of man power, not only for building dykes and earthworks but also, on a mammoth scale, in transportation, in the manufacture of engineering materials, and in commissariat. In Anhwei province alone some 914,000 rural workers were engaged temporarily in transportation during the first year of the project. The supplying of food and fuel to this tremendous corps of workers involves a complicated liaison between the provincial and central governments. In 1952 some 430,000 industrial workers worked hard to ensure a steady flow of engineering materials—from screws, nuts, and bolts to sluice gates.

"You see," said Chien, "the labour and direction are entirely Chinese. It is true that there is a Russian adviser; but he advises on water engineering works throughout our country and is not specifically attached to the Hwai River project."

She insisted that even the materials used came from within the country, except some pile-driving machines (from Russia) and a few tractors and lorries (mostly from Czechoslovakia). Concrete mixers, which had been imported from the United States, were now manufactured in Shanghai. Sluice gates, which had been purchased from Germany, Britain, and America, were now made in China.

"Ours," said Chien, her eyes shining, "is a triumph of Chinese manual labour."

Soviet engineering methods have influenced some aspects of construction. The Lung Ho-chi dam, for instance, has a foundation on the Russian lateral model consisting of a block or blanket of nonpermeable clay, about twenty-five feet thick, and projecting some forty feet on the upstream side. On the downstream side are inverted filters of fine sand and coarse rubble. This system obviates the use of vertical steel sheets, thus saving some expenditure in steel and wood. It had worked very well, said Chien.

At the Hwai River project, as elsewhere, the Communists by high-lighting individual performance inspire collective effort. The individual worker is made to feel that his contribution to the collective pool is separately valued and rewarded. During the first year of construction some 24,600 model workers were elected and honoured. Incidentally, there are about 220,000 women workers, and some 3,000 of them have been elected model workers.

Three instruments are principally employed for mobilising the people's cooperation, and the incentive for each proceeds from the 40,000 cadres, or politically dependable party officials, who are attached to the project. Patriotic Emulation Drives seek to stir the competitive spirit and thereby increase output. Research is encouraged by the Patriotic Technical Study Groups, while the Patriotic Pact Inspection Group ensures that pacts for stepping up production and remedying defects and deficiencies are implemented. The Communists are quick to compare their own efforts with those of the Kuomintang, whose multipurpose projects they denounce as being designed primarily for the benefit of the landlords. Yet characteristically they have retained a few engineers of the Kuomintang regime on the Hwai project. The State is prepared to use whoever is willing to serve it.

By and large the hydroelectric power which this project will generate is of modest proportions. Many of us remarked on this, and Chien explained why it was so.

"It's largely a matter of geography," she said. "In the Hwai River area the tributaries and streams are numerous. They spread like the ribs of a fan over this region. On the other hand, the valleys for storage and reservoir are few and far between. There are in fact no large valleys. Ultimately it's a question of priorities. Between power generation and flood protection the latter comes first."

By 1955, when the project is completed, there will be twenty-one reservoirs holding collectively about six and one-half billion cubic yards of water. In addition there will be seventeen lakes with a storage capacity of nineteen and one-half billion cubic yards. Four new navigation lines extending over some twelve hundred miles will be navigable to motor boats of 300 tons.

A thin drizzle descended as our barges turned homeward, and the Lung Ho-chi dam looked like a blurred print in the haze. I thought that Chien, having accomplished Operation Hwai, would be more relaxed. We tried to draw her out, to get her to speak about herself and to expound on matters more animated than charts; but she would not thaw.

Here was the Communist incarnate, the "sea-green incorruptible" who, wedded to her own creed, looked with amused disdain on our bourgeois pattern of life. She seemed no more to understand our jargon than we could reconcile ourselves to her Marxist idiom. Obviously she was not interested in individuals as individuals—not even in herself. When one among us asked what was the most exciting experience in her career as a Communist and an engineer, she solemnly retailed an incident when the work schedule threatened to go awry on the Hwai River project. The engineers were baffled by a problem. It was the workers finally who provided the answer.

"That," said Chien at the end of a breathless ten-minute recital, "was one of the most exciting experiences of my life."

Yet her career was packed with incident. Her father was an American-trained engineer. She herself had studied engineering at Shanghai University, where as a Communist student she had attracted the attention of the Japanese authorities. In her last year at the University she decided to escape to the "liberated areas." There she learned more engineering from practical experience than her textbooks had taught her. She loved her work, but her god was Marx.

Did she see her work in terms of the people or only in terms of the omnipotent, inanimate State? In her vocabulary all things were subordinate to the leadership of the Communist party. Despite her occasional expansiveness and her quick smile, she was somehow hard and flintlike.

Around us the river swarmed with life. A family of four paddled past in a skiff. Great rectangular sails billowed in the breeze. Along the water's edge other craft laboured heavily against the wind and thin lines of men and women strained at the ropes as they drew the junks along the banks. Their feet squelched in the muddy swamp, and the veins stood knotted on their necks and foreheads. And of a sudden the symbolism of the scene struck me. Were the river and the people really harnessed as one, as Chien Chen-ying claimed? The whole burden of the Hwai seemed to rest on the bent, straining backs of these grunting fisherfolk. Would the load lessen and the strain ease as the sails caught the breeze again? Or, like Sinbad with the Old Man of the Sea, would the burden on their tired shoulders grow?

8

MÄDCHEN IN UNIFORM

"The People's Republic of China," reads Article 6 of the Common Programme, "shall abolish the feudal system which holds women in bondage. Women shall enjoy equal rights with men in political, economic, cultural, educational, and social life. Freedom of marriage for men and women shall be put into effect."

This was adopted by the first plenary session of the Chinese People's Political Consultative Conference on September 29, 1949. Seven months later the new Marriage Law came into force, on May 1, 1950.

Of the many changes noticeable under the Red regime few strike the visitor more than the altered status of women. Looking back to Chungking in 1944, I cannot recall a single serious conversation I had with a Chinese woman save with Madame Sun Yat-sen. The women of the Kuomintang regime were certainly more decorative than the women of Mao's China. They were sleek and coiffured, and the flash of silks and brocades gave colour to the drab khaki of wartime Chungking. China today has a strictly utilitarian look, and only Adam in a wicked mood could have devised the regulation uniform of blue cotton coat and trousers which Eve flaunts in the garden of Red Cathay.

Clothes may make the man, as our bourgeois sartorial artists insist. But in China they do not make the woman. Despite uniform attire China's women are today more alert, active, and alive than they ever were in the two decades of Chiang's rule. Vaguely in the old Chungking of Kuomintang days one heard of Madame Chiang Kai-shek's New Life movement—or the No Life movement, as it was more widely known. There are movements also in Mao's China, but of a different genre.

I found myself comparing India and China in the altered status of women. Both had changed under the stress of political battle, and the revolution of Gandhi no less than the revolution of Mao had lit a fire in millions of feminine minds. Eve was emancipated. But the tempo and form of the movements in the two countries differed noticeably.

Because few trends illustrate more graphically the differences between the democratic and the totalitarian outlook, the two movements merit close study. In the course of helping to break their country's political chains India's women broke many of the social shackles which encumbered them. But not all. The paradox of feminine emancipation in India is that, while women are increasingly prominent in the professions and in the country's political life, the vast majority of them do not enjoy equal rights with their menfolk in marriage, divorce, and inheritance. Only in certain areas, such as Malabar, Travancore, and Cochin, where matriliny is the rule, do Indian women have equal rights with men.

Monogamy, though in practice the rule, is not theoretically recognised by Hinduism. Islam also permits polygamy to the extent of four wives; but this is conditional on the husband's ability to deal equitably with his spouses. Divorce is unknown to Hindu sacramental marriage. Under the Dissolution of Muslim Marriages Act, 1939, a Muslim woman may obtain a decree dissolving her marriage on certain grounds—neglect, cruelty, desertion for four years, disease, etc. But she does not enjoy the arbitrary male prerogative of pronouncing talak (divorce) without assigning any reason whatever. Moreover Hindu widows and Hindu women generally have no absolute estate over the property which they inherit as heirs. Under Islamic law, a Muslim woman does not lose her interest in the family property on her marriage. A Hindu woman does.

Since the achievement of independence attempts have been made in India to erase these inequalities. The Hindu Code Bill was introduced in Parliament with this object, and Pandit Nehru was known to favour it; but orthodox, vested interests forced its withdrawal.

In feminine emancipation China has at one vault leaped several centuries. About the only visible relic of the medieval past is the microscopic bound feet of a few women, the youngest of whom are in their late fifties. Equality was the keynote in the Communist-held areas, and with the comradeship of battle the bond grew. Nevertheless, old habits die hard, as even the Communists admit. In an article in the magazine *People's China* of June, 1952, the Minister of Justice, Madame Shih Liang, discusses the difficulties frankly. "It must be acknowledged," she writes, "that the reactionary feudal marriage system of China whose origin dates back thousands of years has a deep-rooted influence on the masses that cannot be swept away within a short period of time. We must use and are using every possible means to implement the Marriage Law thoroughly."

What was not immediately practicable in democratic India was achieved overnight in totalitarian China. True, the Common Programme was the handiwork of the Chinese People's Political Consultative Conference, which might loosely be described as China's hand-picked Parliament. The mechanism of Communism enables a regime to clamp on a social and economic revolution immediately in the wake of a political upheaval. In India's Parliament the opposition of the orthodox or "reactionary" interests forced the government to withdraw the Hindu Code Bill. In

China's "Parliament" the problem was simplified by having these "reactionary" elements arbitrarily excluded.

The emancipation of China's women must help considerably two of the Communist regime's primary objectives: the dissolution of the old family system, and the harnessing of a new, vastly vital force to the dedicated service of the State.

In the traditional society of ancient China women occupied a subservient place. Confucius visualised society as made up of five relationships: ruler and subject, husband and wife, father and son, elder brothers and younger, and friends. According to the Sage, there was rule on the one side of the first four and submission on the other. Relations between friends were on the basis of the mutual promotion of virtue. Confucius held that chastity and docility were the characteristics of a good woman. Although he mourned his mother's death he spoke rarely, and never generously, about women.

By equating women with men in all departments, including the domestic, Mao's regime has struck a resounding blow at the basis of Chinese society and simultaneously has mobilised new friends and allies to its support. Five elements characterise the Communists' marriage law: free choice of partners, monogamy, the complete equality of the sexes, equal rights of divorce, and the protection of the legitimate interests of women and children.

These are revolutionary changes, and in the Communist reckoning their impact on the old order will be as important as that of the agrarian reforms. "As the agrarian reform sets free hundreds of millions of landless and land-hungry peasants from oppression by the feudal landlords, so the Marriage Law marks the emancipation of the Chinese women from the feudal marriage system under which they were utterly bereft of any rights." *

Briefly, the Law sets the minimum age for marriage at twenty for men and eighteen for women. It forbids marriage in certain circumstances, e.g., where the man and the woman are lineal

---

* Foreword to the Marriage Law of The People's Republic of China (Foreign Languages Press, Peking).

relatives by blood, in the case of half-brothers and half-sisters, where one party is sexually impotent, or where one party is suffering from venereal disease, mental disease, or leprosy. Children born out of wedlock are accorded the same rights as children born in lawful wedlock. Under Article 7, "husband and wife are companions living together and shall enjoy equal status in the home."

Divorce is automatically granted when husband and wife both desire it. Both are required to register with the subdistrict people's government in order to obtain the necessary certificates. After establishing that both desire divorce and that "appropriate measures have been taken for the care of children and property," the subdistrict people's government is required to issue the divorce certificates "without delay."

Where only one party insists on divorce the procedure is slightly different. In the first instance, the subdistrict people's government and the subdistrict judicial organ shall try to effect a reconciliation. If they fail the case must be referred without delay to the district or city people's court for decision. This court must again try to bring about a reconciliation; if unsuccessful, it must render a verdict without delay.

A husband is forbidden to apply for divorce if his wife is with child. This restriction does not operate in the case of a woman seeking divorce. After divorce the duty of supporting and educating the children devolves on both parents. Both parties are required to reach an agreement on the amount and duration of maintenance and education. If they fail to reach an agreement the People's Court decides.

In Peking I attended a People's Court and listened to two divorce cases. Both were concerned with peasant couples. In the first case the woman, who was pregnant, was suing for divorce from her husband on the ground that he was seeing too much of his first wife. The couple had three children. On the podium was the presiding judge, a man, flanked on the right by a representative of the All-China Democratic Women's Federation who

appeared to act in the combined role of jury and counsel for the
wife. Officially she was called the People's Representative. To the
left of the judge sat another woman who acted as court clerk.

The procedure was extremely informal, each party to the suit
answering questions asked by the judge. Both the judge and the
People's Representative then spoke, each advising the two parties
to be reconciled for the sake of the children. Their appeal was
successful, and husband and wife agreed to try again. I watched
them walking stolidly out of the dingy courtroom into the sunlight. They strode out of the gate together.

In the second case the presiding judge was replaced by a
capable, intelligent-looking woman. The other two women remained. Here again the wife was suing the husband for divorce.
They were young, sturdy peasants with square strong hands and
weather-beaten faces. The marriage had been an orthodox, arranged match of the old-fashioned type, and the woman, pleading
coercion when married, asked for divorce on that ground. The
husband was willing, but the wife's share of property was the
point in dispute. She asked for two mus, roughly one-third of an
acre. The man, who argued that he was supporting his parents,
and that the division of his property would make the remainder
uneconomic, offered 800 catties (960 pounds) of rice instead. The
woman refused. The judge decided that she should have her two
mus. They walked out of the court separately.

"A wife married is like a horse bought," runs an old Chinese
saying. If China knows no other freedom her women now at least
know freedom in the choice of their partners. In the first four
months of the Marriage Law the number of divorce applications
in fifteen large and small cities more than doubled that of the
previous four months. Applications by women accounted for 70
to 90 per cent of the total. In rural areas the figures also showed
a tendency to increase.

Alongside the freeing from old and oppressive bonds came an
increase in the number of "free choice marriages." Of 400 marriages registered in the first half of 1951 in 178 villages in the

Hwailai county of Chahar province, 311 were arranged by the parties themselves. The second half of 1951 revealed an even larger proportion of free-choice marriages. The current Chinese saying runs: "One unhappy couple has turned into two loving pairs."

If the social status of the Chinese woman was strengthened by the Marriage Law her economic equality was emphasised by the agrarian reform. Women who never previously had the right to own land are now assured of their own share of the soil by the Agrarian Reform law. For the first time in many thousands of years the Chinese peasant witnesses the phenomenon of his wife and daughters holding the same share of land as he does. Not only that. They also enjoy the same rights in its disposal. Confronted with these facts which give reality to the new status of women the peasants recognise that the position of their wives and daughters both in the family and in society has undergone a radical change. Nothing has done more to revolutionise the face of rural China. Inevitably it has made women the spearhead of the land reform movement.

The Communists early argued that the emancipation of women must make for the emancipation and good of the entire Chinese society. Women might not always control the direction of progress, but invariably they influenced its tempo. It was endemic in the speed of the Chinese revolution that, having "arrived" so suddenly, it should go forward on its own momentum. No single factor has so accelerated the pace of progress as the grant of equal status to China's women.

Eve's healing and quickening touch is seen in all fields. With equality for women the status of children has improved. The health, welfare, and education of all Chinese children has become a major concern of the State. "Public health and medical work," says Article 48 of the Common Programme, "shall be expanded, and attention shall be paid to the protection of the health of mothers, infants, and children."

In this task the government is helped greatly by the All-China

Democratic Women's Federation which was set up shortly after the meeting of the First All-China Women's Congress in 1949. The Federation works through a network of women's representative conferences spread throughout the country and its roll early in 1952 disclosed more than 76,000,000 members. Characteristically it is organised in rural areas on a village basis and in cities on a street basis.

Child care has made impressive progress in the past three years. The Communists say that the crèches and nurseries set up by factories, government organisations, and schools exceed 1,220, which is nine times the number before liberation. Apart from these there are seasonal nurseries, and in 1952 more than 500,000 children of working parents were said to have benefited from crèche and nursery care, or school education.

In mid-April, 1952, the Chinese government placed the number of children's hospitals in the country at 156. Apart from this, more than 700 women's and children's health stations and nearly 1,000 maternity service stations were, it was claimed, set up throughout China in towns, industrial suburbs, rural districts, subdistricts, and villages. During the past two years Chinese figures reveal that well over 150,000,000 children were vaccinated against smallpox and nearly a million received BCG inoculations against tuberculosis as well as against diphtheria and whooping cough.

The training of health and medical personnel is being expedited, as we discovered on our visit to the Medical University of North China in Mukden. Even allowing for exaggeration—and Chinese figures in the Kuomintang regime were also inflated—the progress made on the health welfare front is not unimpressive. The Peking University Medical College has now a department for mother and child health studies. A new Women's and Children's Health College has been opened in Mukden. Alongside these expanding facilities for modern medical training, local centres are retraining old-fashioned midwives on a fairly large scale.

How far child and maternal mortality have benefited from these developments it is difficult to discover. A writer in the March–April, 1952, number of the bimonthly *China Reconstructs* quotes the death rate from infant tetanus in Hoche district of Pingyuan province as having fallen from 42 per cent to 1 per cent. But he omits to note over what period. Nor is it easy to calculate how the Communists can produce the requisite personnel to run these greatly expanded services, despite the expedited training courses and other short-term measures.

Women work alongside men in every department of China's variegated life. Some 650,000 women workers are employed in various industries. These comprise scientists, technicians, engineers, factory managers and directors, tram drivers, train conductors, train crew and ordinary industrial workers. More than three-fifths of the workers in the textile industry are women. Many of these women have won distinction as model workers, and some like Hao Chien-hsiu, who established a new record for reducing waste cotton entangled in rollers, and Chang Shu-yun, who invented an advanced operational method of packing cigarettes, are household names.

The Patriotic Movement for Bumper Crops saw women in the forefront of the rural drive. In Pingyuan province in North China one-third of the agricultural model workers are said to be women. In Northeast China female labour is extensively deployed on the fields in order to release male peasants for work in mines and factories. Women are also actively engaged in auxiliary and handicraft production. Several thousands—one estimate places them at 650,000—have helped their menfolk in the channel clearing work on the Yellow, the Yangtze, and the Yi rivers. Another 220,000 are cited as having worked on the dykes of the Hwai River project.

There are women in the people's army, navy, and air force. Some have qualified as parachutists. There are women railroad engineers, doctors, teachers, nurses, officials, and ministers. At least 600,000 women rank as members of the Chinese Communist party, whose number is now believed to approximate five million.

We met at least two prominent Chinese women writers, Ting Ling and Tsao Ming. Tsao, whom we saw in Mukden, is small, slight, gravely diffident, with a rare but attractive smile. She is best known for her novel *The Moving Force* which is set against the industrial background of a Manchuria peopled by cruel Japanese, crafty Kuomintang agents, and patriotic if sometimes naïve Communists. Ting Ling, short, dumpy, with a gay plump face—the "moon face" beloved of China's poets—comes from Mao's Hunan and is renowned for her short stories. We saw her at more than one reception at Peking, and it would be difficult to guess from her lively, observant eyes that here is a woman who has known hardship and tragedy.

Government absorbs a goodly proportion of Chinese women. Like the men, the women of New China have the right to elect and be elected to public office. One of China's six Vice-Chairmen is a woman, Madame Sun Yat-sen.

Madame Sun was matronly when I met her in Chungking nine years ago, but carried the delicate suggestion of peach blossoms and porcelain. Alas, since then the matron has achieved the amplitude of the matriarch. In her office at Shanghai where she greeted us she proved to be a dowager dressed dowdily in black. In Chungking she had conversed in English. Now she murmured polite platitudes in Chinese with an accent which the interpreter obviously had difficulty in disentangling. On one wall was a caricature of Mr. Acheson as a tentacled bug holding a parchment of peace in one hand and hugging a container of bacterial bugs in the other. Madame Sun pointed to the drawing and laughed. On the walls also hung portraits of Stalin, Lenin, Marx, and Engels. Mao was flanked by Chu Teh. But where was Sun Yat-sen?

In all, thirty-six women hold important positions in the higher echelons of the Central People's Government, including two ministers. Madame Li Teh-chuan, a mild, mousy-mannered, pleasant-speaking woman who looks like a picture of your favourite aunt, is Minister of Health. Sitting at the same table with her at one of the numerous banquets in Peking, I got her talking on bacterial warfare. She told me she had gone to Korea to investigate the matter, and spoke with genuine earnestness. I was not convinced; but, whatever the rights or wrongs of the case, she obviously felt deeply about it. A silent listener at that table was General Wu Hsiu-chuan, who had led Communist China's delegation to the United Nations in November, 1950.

Another listener was Madame Kung Peng, whom I met often in her capacity as director of the Press Bureau of the Foreign Office. An attractive, intelligent woman, she is well versed in political matters and speaks English fluently. Hearing that I had been in Chungking during the war she once remarked that she had also been there—on a Communist newspaper. The only other personal remark she ventured was a reference to her sister who had been in India en route to the United States. Kung Peng had potential liveliness as a conversationalist, but she was careful never to scintillate. One morning with my journalist colleague, Chalapathi Rau, I called on her at the Foreign Office for an official interview. We were shown into a room, and shortly after Kung Peng entered with two Chinese, a man and a woman. We greeted her in English. She replied distantly in Chinese. The man, it turned out, was an interpreter, and the woman faithfully recorded the entire conversation. Although the interpreter's English was indifferent and he often floundered, Kung Peng only once lapsed into English. This was to elucidate her answer to a question on the mass executions of 1950.

The other woman minister in the government is Madame Shih Liang, Minister of Justice. In the drab hierarchy of Communist China she strikes a decorative note. Always elegantly garbed, usually in a tailored white linen suit, she wears lipstick and carries herself with an air. I heard that she had confessed during the San Fan movement to a weakness for decorating her office with flowers!

Another notable figure is Chou En-lai's wife, better known by her own name, Teng Ying-chao. She is Vice-Chairman of the All-China Women's Democratic Federation and an alternate member of the party's Central Committee, or Politburo. She took part in the Long March and is a veteran in party-sponsored women's activities. Madame Teng looks older than her sprightly husband, but there is grace still in her faintly regal carriage.

Women also figure in the provincial People's Government Councils where they constitute over 4 per cent of the total membership. There are said to be 287 women members. In municipal and village governments the feminine proportion is perceptibly larger. Of the 220 municipal members of the sixteen district governments under the city of Peking, 35 are women—16 per cent of the total. In the village governments of the thirteen hsiens (or counties) of the Hsüchang district in Honan more than 1,000 women cadres (party officials) are of peasant origin. More than 500 women of various national minorities serve as cadres in the people's governments at chu (district) or hsien level in Sinkiang province. A district, incidentally, is a subdivision of a county.

Thus women are rapidly infiltrating into the country's public life and a large number of activists—that is, workers and leaders who inspire activity, have emerged from the feminine masses. China's women have taken a vigorous part in various national movements, notably the campaign for Resisting American Aggression and Aiding Korea. They have encouraged their sons and husbands to volunteer for service in Korea and simultaneously they have canvassed signatures for a Five-Power Peace Pact. Many among them have served with the Volunteer Medical Corps and the Volunteer Surgical Corps amid the shambles and bloodshed of Korea. From them the New China derives much of her sustenance and stimulus.

Human nature changes slowly, and even the volcanic change brought about in the Chinese woman's status has not altogether eradicated the Eve in her. On a railway platform at Mukden I watched an old peasant woman talking to her soldier son. She was taller than most of the women around her, and she stood, despite her age, very slim and erect and proud. The wind blew her soft white wispy hair like an aureole around her head. Her deep sunken eyes were tranquil but sad, and lines creased a face which I thought must once have been marmoreal in its beauty. She seemed to be whispering to her son. And all of a sudden through her sadness she smiled. The smile lit her face with a strange radiance and, looking at her, I was reminded of the mother of the Gracchi.

9

WHAT PRICE CULTURE?

Near Tatung is a Buddhist temple, the first religious centre we visited in China. Three black-robed monks fluttered like jackdaws at the doorway.

Before entering the temple we asked whether we should remove our shoes as is customary at most shrines of Asia. Our guides brusquely told us not to do so.

The temple itself was a riot of colour inside. A row of gleaming Buddhas sat on the steps of an altar lacquered in red and gold. From the ceiling hung tall sacred scrolls. The walls were covered with murals, and brass urns and vases lit the dim recesses of the interior. Save for these embellishments there was nothing religious about the place. It had the atmosphere of a museum rather than a temple. No monks chanted their hymns, though later at a shrine in Peking I saw an old monk intoning his prayers. Not a wisp of incense coiled in the air. We saw no worshippers.

Emerging into the courtyard, one of us inquired whether any incense sticks were available to light before the Buddha. There were none. Where were the sacred books? They were stored in another temple—no one had worshipped here for two or three years. How did the monks subsist?

"We have some land," said one of the timid trio, "and the government also assists us."

Despite their abject desire to please—and to be rid of us—it was difficult not to sympathise with the monks. As we stood around them, jostled by our guides, they broke into a stylized tribute to the regime. The wicked Kuomintang, they complained, had stacked ammunition in the temple. Chiang's soldiery had desecrated the place; but Mao's regime allowed them freedom of worship, and the government took good care of the temple. The Communists had painted the temple gate and tidied up its precincts.

Oddly enough, almost the same tribute rolled from the lips of a Mongolian monk at the Lama temple at Peking. There, as at Ta Tung, was the flurry of black robes. But the Peking recitation differed in one particular: Chiang had not stacked his ammunition at this temple—he had committed the more heinous sin of quartering his troops.

The only Christian church I entered in China was one at Pengpu, stripped of altars and images and serving as the exhibition hall for the Hwai River project. Even so, the Gothic windows, aisles and façade betrayed plainly its original purpose.

From a foreign diplomat in Peking—a man of much charm and urbane wit—I learned of a New Reformed Church, the Communist counterpart of the Old Catholic Church, where posters on bacteriological warfare and Communist slogans draped the walls around the altar in the sanctuary.

The diplomat is a great-great-grandnephew, if I remember rightly, of a Pope. I remarked on this when I first met him.

"Ah, yes," he admitted, his eyes twinkling. "But there's a dark secret in my life. My mother was a Casanova."

There is certainly as much "freedom" of religion in China as there is "freedom" of culture. But both are hedged by one paramount limitation. Such freedom can operate only within the bounds prescribed by the Communist party and along the lines laid down by the government.

Culture is as the Communists ordain it. "They tell me," said Napoleon once, "that France has no literature. I must speak to the Minister of the Interior about it." In much the same way the path of literature and the arts is carefully charted by the Communists, who here, as elsewhere, will tolerate no deviation.

A revealing glimpse into the attitude of China's rulers towards art is provided by the comment of Chou Yang, a noted literary critic now Vice-Minister of Cultural Affairs, on the story "Old Worker Kuo Fu-shan" by a pro-Communist writer in *People's Literature*. The story tells how a tried Communist worker, overcome by physical fear of bombing, is cured of his neurosis by his old father, who is not a member of the party. Both father and son become heroes.

Chou Yang fumes against the story: "Obviously the author not only distorts the image of a model Party member, but also completely ignores the function of Party training and leadership. It appears that a model Party member was inferior to an ordinary old workman; that at a critical moment a man's behaviour was decided not by the level of political understanding which he had attained, but by the physical, mental defects and abnormalities resulting from a certain cause; that the violent and vicious acts of the imperialists could scare the Chinese workers; that a Party member's education was corrected not by Party education, but by his father's influence. Throughout the incident, the decisive factor is the physical one, not the political one. The family relation is the important one, not his relation to the Party. Is it not obvious that such a work, from the point of view of its political and ideological content, is entirely erroneous?" *

The lines which govern Red China's literary production are contained in Mao Tse-tung's "Address at the Yenan Round Table Discussion on Literature and Art," published in May, 1942. This

---

* For Chou Yang's comment, see *Chinese Literature*, No. 1 (Autumn, 1951—The Cultural Press, Peking), pp. 5–18. For the story, "Old Worker Kuo Fu-shan," by Ting Ke-sing, see *People's Literature*, Vol. IV, No. 1.

is now recognised in China as the Bible of all good Communist writers and artists. Mao poses and answers two questions.

The first is: "Whom are literature and art to serve?" The answer to this is unequivocal. They should serve "the workers, peasants and soldiers." The second question is: "How to serve them?" Broadly this should be achieved by writers and artists identifying themselves with the worker-soldier-peasant masses.

Of all social elements the Communist is most suspicious of the "petty bourgeois intelligentsia." In his reckoning these elements, although revolutionary because of their indigent circumstances, are not ideologically sound. To them belong the majority of writers and artists who believe that, because they sympathise with the working people, they should automatically be identified with the proletariat. This is heresy. "Economically," said Lenin long before Mao, "the intelligentsia has no conflict with the proletariat. Nevertheless, in living conditions and in labour, it is non-proletarian. Hence, there is conflict between them psychologically and ideologically."

To neutralise and erase this conflict Mao adjures China's writers and artists to study Marxism-Leninism and to study society. In other words, these elements should submit themselves to ideological remoulding by entering into the actual struggle of the proletariat and, in the process, should slough off their nonproletarian ideology. They should throw themselves into the struggle of the masses "permanently, unconditionally, and whole-heartedly."

This line is called "the class line and the mass line in literature." Without such identification between the literary class and the masses, say the Communists, artistic creation "would be severed from its sources and writers and artists would lose the basis for their ideological reformation."

China's contemporary art and literature may embrace the different thoughts and trends of the Four Friendly Classes—the proletariat, the peasantry, the petty bourgeoisie, and the national bourgeoisie—but "it should be guided by proletarian ideology, Marxism-Leninism, and Mao Tse-tung's teachings."

Inevitably literature and the arts tend to follow the Communist pattern, the writer and the painter working with one eye on their fellow workers and the other on the party. To deviate from the strait and narrow path is to sin against the light. There can be no departing from the masses and from reality. Otherwise the realm of Red literature and art will be invaded and contaminated "by bourgeois and petty-bourgeois ideas." So the Communists warn.

In the New China it is the primary duty of the artist and the writer to depict the new qualities of the new people—to portray the Chinese people, in Mao Tse-tung's historic phrase, "standing on their own feet." This implies the extolling of Communist deeds and Communist virtues and the denunciation of all "reactionary" trends. In the process all that is worth while in China's old cultural heritage should be preserved; but the "feudal dregs" must be scraped off. Mao calls upon his followers to distinguish between the products of the old-time feudal ruling class and the old-time folk culture. Old popular art forms in ballads, plays, dances, and operas should be turned to new uses.

China's best-known folk opera, *The White-Haired Girl*, marks the first attempt to create a musical drama in a *yang-ko* framework. The *yang-ko* is a traditional peasant-dance performed to the drum-and-gong beat of a planting song. Working on this theme, the Communists have evolved a people's new *yang-ko* which has influenced nearly every vehicle of artistic creation in the country. New dance forms like "Production Dance" and "Dance of the Advancing Army" are among its first fruits. The *yang-ko* also provides a popular motif for Peking's famous handicrafts, notably for cloisonné ware. New designs have invaded this field and with them porcelain and jade and ivory carvings have acquired original and vigorous forms.

Within this rigid groove the Communists are prepared to look both backward and forward. In the Tunhwang caves in Kansu, on the edge of the Gobi Desert, are murals dating from A.D. 366. The majority of these deal with religious themes, but a number depict the daily life of the people. There are scenes of farming, fighting, hunting, and jousting. Chinese craftsmen are now cleverly transferring these designs to trays, vases, lamps, powder boxes, tea containers, and rugs. Today the Tunhwang patterns vie in popularity with the peace dove of Picasso and the gay *yang-ko* silhouettes of boy dancing with girl.

Any departure from reality and the masses is anathema. Art is rooted in the people and must draw its sustenance from them. Mao would have his countrymen derive inspiration from their rich cultural heritage so long as they do not stray from the narrow path of proletarian virtue and lapse into bourgeois heresy and decay. In his book *The Chinese Revolution and the Chinese Communist Party*, Mao warns his followers that "it is not permissible to dress up as revolutionary heroes the reactionaries in history." Peter the Great can no more be compared to Lenin than can the great Manchu, Ch'ien Lung, to Mao Tse-tung. Did not Stalin remark: "Peter the Great is only as a drop of water in the ocean whilst Lenin is as the whole boundless ocean itself"?

We were told of new writers springing from among the worker-peasant masses. How effective or popular they are, only those conversant with Chinese language or literature can tell. A feature of the new writings dating from the days when the Communists were cribbed, cabined, and confined within the Liberated Areas is the atmosphere of ardent struggle which permeates them. As Chou Yang observes in *The People's New Literature*, "heroes are not born but they are made heroes in the forge of battle." Representative of this new mass school of writers is Cheng Teng-ko, who apparently learned to read and write only after joining the Liberation Army. Among his better known works are *Mrs. Tu* and *Living Hell*.

Red resourcefulness exploits every vehicle of cultural expression for its own rigid purpose. Drama in China is too often melodrama. While following traditional patterns in that villain, hero, and heroines are starkly drawn, old folk forms are not merely being adapted to new political purposes; in the process they are themselves undergoing a technical metamorphosis. "In adapting old forms," said Lu Hsun, posthumously worshipped as the sage of modern China, "some things must be eliminated. What has been eliminated must be replaced. The result is the appearance of a new form, and that is change."

Revenge, for instance, is the main motif of plays such as *The White-Haired Girl,* which constitutes a major invocation to hate. In this it conforms to Communist dogma which rests on the two props of hatred for one's opponent and loyalty to one's creed. Song, music, ballad, opera, and dance, all are harnessed to this elementary, elemental purpose.

The Peking opera with its high, stilted falsetto singing survives, but the themes it portrays are now attuned to the altered tempo of the times. "Our duty," says a Communist writer, "is to restore the true significance of history and to create new historical drama according to the concepts of historical materialism, so that the old-form drama will give the masses a new and scientific interpretation of history."

We saw several operas and concerts including a performance by the fifty-eight-year-old Mei Lan-fang, China's most celebrated operatic star. Mei appeared with his son in a Peking opera entitled *Love in Dream,* a gentle fantasy set in a peony pavilion peopled by ethereal beings such as the Goddess of the Garden and the Goddess of Flowers. It was all very lovely and languid, with nothing proletarian about it; but other Peking operas, notably *Three Attacks on Chu Chia Village,* have a robust Marxist motif.

Included in the same programme were three short operettas set in the Ming and Ch'ing periods. One of these, *Fight at an Inn,* was a lively acrobatic affair while the masks and music in another, *The Stolen Imperial Horse,* were curiously reminiscent of the Kathakali dances of South India. Shanta, watching in dreamy ecstasy, was entranced.

At Shanghai we sampled more versions of Chinese opera, including the Shao-hsing opera, which again is geared to the dogmas of the regime. Local variants also include the Shensi and Peng-peng, and all are having their old forms adapted to new moulds.

The cinema is a comparatively new form of art to the Communists, who for many years were prevented by circumstances from exploiting it. Inevitably *The White-Haired Girl* was among the earliest movie products, and in Peking the pleasant-faced actress who portrayed the heroine was a guest at more than one reception we attended. By and large Chinese films are no great advertisement for the celluloid art. Like their Indian counterparts, they tend to drag, and the propaganda overtones often have crude effects more suited to a Wild West melodrama than to a serious drama. Yet amusingly enough Chinese producers insist that their products meticulously eschew "the Hollywood influence."

Among the films I saw was *Inner Mongolian People's Victory*, a tedious and ineffectual compromise between documentary and drama. At Shanghai we saw a documentary of the San Fan trial held at Peking early in the year. It displayed some of the sadistic scenes enacted at this judicial carnival. We saw close-ups of the trembling accused, who, manacled hand and foot, were hustled onto a huge stage by armed guards while the mob, led by cheer-leaders, bayed for their blood. The Finance Minister, Po Yi-po, who read the indictment, figured prominently in the picture, and sentence was finally pronounced by the diminutive Chief Justice of the Supreme Court, whose "gallery" on the platform included the elegant woman Minister of Justice, Madame Shih Liang. The film, incidentally, was introduced by a speaker who recited a slogan which governed the people's justice in this case: "To be lenient, to be strict. To be lenient to the majority, strict to the minority. To be lenient to those who confess, to be strict to those who do not." Two out of the seven accused were sentenced to death. Two were acquitted. The remaining three were condemned to imprisonment for varying terms.

Despite their patterned presentation, the many concerts we attended rarely palled. Meticulous attention was paid to décor and lighting, and the general effect was pleasing, if stylized. China's new songs have a buoyant, vibrant lilt though some appear to be modelled on Central European airs and one at least echoed the resonant roll of the Volga Boatmen's Song. How like puppets a Chinese chorus look on the stage, their tiny mouths opening in strange birdlike movements with a flash of gleaming teeth! Surely there was nothing of the inscrutable Oriental about them. They smiled with their mouths and eyes.

Painting is perhaps the only art which has most obviously withered and wilted under the Communist touch. With rare exceptions such as the shrimps, flowers, and fruits of the nonagenarian Chi Pai-shih, the form and colour of most modern Chinese paintings are wooden and lifeless. Even Chi's paintings, technically superb, are often stilted.

Chi himself is a venerable picturesque figure with a thin wispy beard, his lean frame encased in a robe and his tremulous hands gripping a lacquered red shepherd's crook. He came to more than one reception in Peking. Chi is "lionised" by the Communists, and with memories of long years of neglect under the Manchus he is sensitive enough to return the compliment.

"Why do you respect the Communists?" one of us asked him.

"Because they respect me," said Chi simply.

Bendre, the artist member of our group, was interesting on Communist China's painters. He thought that Chinese artists, uncertain of the Communist mood, were still groping and hesitant. As a result their drawing was almost photographic, their use of colour purely decorative, and their paintings tended to look like flat, flashy oleographs.

They also flattered the Russians by imitation.

"Have you noticed," asked Bendre, "how much Chinese posters resemble the Russian? I have a feeling that very often they merely substitute Chinese faces for Russian."

Bendre felt that the explanation for this static phase was that the artist in China now dedicated himself to purely practical tasks. Painting had hitched its wagon to a utilitarian star. The Chinese painter had only three outlets. He could be a teacher of art. Or he might take to political themes as a painter of prominent leaders or of episodes glorifying the regime. Or he might turn to the painting of stage scenes, the designing of costumes, décor, or choreography. In any of the three fields he was generally reluctant to experiment.

Would the Chinese emerge from this phase?

"It's difficult to tell," said Bendre. "The Russians have still to do it."

There is nothing vandalistic in the new regime's attitude to the country's cultural movements. Indeed the Communists have always carefully emphasised the need to respect and preserve China's artistic treasures. "Protect cultural monuments" was among their earliest slogans.

This is in line with the teaching of Mao in his book *New Democracy*. "China," he writes, "created a glorious culture of the old time in its feudal society that lasted for a long period. . . . But we should by no means take over everything uncritically. Instead we should distinguish all rotten things of the old-time feudal ruling class from the old-time folk culture, and from the things that are more or less democratic or revolutionary."

It is interesting to see how Mao sees common strands in the long thread of China's story. "The new politics and new economy of present-day China," he argues, "are developments of the old politics and old economy of ancient times. The new culture of present-day China is a development of the old culture of ancient times. Therefore we should respect our history and on no account cut ourselves off from it."

Here then is the rationale behind the Communists' eager desire to preserve the country's cultural monuments. These monuments are now not only the people's heritage but the people's possession. "This is the property of the Chinese people. Respect it," runs a signboard in one of Peking's numerous parks.

Equally significant was the comment by the guide who showed us around the majestic Temple of Heaven in the Capital. A beautiful fifteenth century structure, crowned with lapis lazuli tiles, it is a dream in symmetry. "This," said the guide with a spacious wave of the hand, "is the creative work of China's labouring classes." The people's possession is also the people's creation.

Of the many cultural centres we visited, none impressed me more than Kü-fow where in the Kung cemetery Confucius lies buried beneath a lofty mound. "The most sagely ancient Teacher, the all-accomplished, all-informed King," reads the inscription on the marble scroll. We visited his temple and house, passing through peaceful courtyards graceful with trees. There were silver apple trees, pomegranates, firs, and a juniper said to have been planted by the sage himself. Beautiful carved stone pillars with writhing dragons sustained the roof. And later we walked through an avenue lined with cypress to the grave of Confucius. I thought of the cedars of Lebanon.

As we drove away in the afternoon sun the fields were green with waving grain, and farmers in blue jeans and straw hats were trundling their one-wheeled carts. Children cheered. Shantung, old and new. The Shantung of Confucius and of Mao. I wondered how the guide would describe him. "The sage of feudal China," he said, "but worthy of our esteem."

Later at Shanghai we were taken around the house of Lu Hsun, described by the guide as "the sage of modern China." He is certainly worthy of Communism's esteem. They call him posthumously "the Gorki of China" though many feel he was nearer Voltaire than the Russian. His portraits reveal a man with a strong face and brooding eyes. Lu Hsun died in 1936. Although not a Communist, he was bitterly and fearlessly critical of the Kuomintang regime; and no writer did more than he, by his fierce satires, to stir in China's youth and intelligentsia a deep smouldering passion and resentment.

We saw the Great Wall of China winding like a rugged massive snake over bleak hills and valleys. We visited Tatung to see the Buddhist caves. They occupy a picturesque site with a garden of white lilac fronting them. And before the caves are curved blue-tiled roofs which gaze on a mud-walled village nestling in the curve of a river with the hills behind. We visited twenty-one out of some four hundred caves, and at least four of these contained giant Buddhas. They lack the monolithic majesty of stone carvings, but their plaster fronts are ablaze with colour. Not all the caves were in good condition. Our guides accused the Kuomintang of neglect. Whatever be the rights and wrongs of the matter, the Communists appear to be making every effort to repair the damage. At Tatung the same night, after a great banquet of fish our hosts presented us with exotic, gaily coloured paper cut-outs, a simple but highly artistic form of folk expression. All were colourful and some most ingenious.

In the Communists, as in Cromwell's Roundheads, is a strong streak of puritanism. This will surprise persons inclined to associate the followers of Marx with licentiousness. In fact the Chinese Communists are puritanical to the point of being prudish. It is said that they have banned fewer plays for political reasons than on moral grounds. Among their other bans is one against male *yang-ko* performers dressing as women. The ban against the too liberal use of cosmetics may be construed as an assault on bourgeois decadence. But it is a strange irony which leads the followers of Marx and Mao to flaunt the banner of Cromwell and the Pilgrim Fathers!

10

ECONOMICS OF LIVING

Currency and Communications were the two C's on which the Communists concentrated shortly after seizing power. If their regime was to register a marked improvement on that of Chiang Kai-shek currency had to be controlled, and communications extended. The two were intertwined. Increased production was one answer to inflation, but unless vital centres could be assured of a steady flow of essential supplies the country's economy would be dislocated. Prices would rise.

In the ultimate analysis economics, not politics, would decide the fate of the regime. Of this the Communists were acutely aware. Unless their rule spelt a better standard of living for the country as a whole, rural and urban, discontent would grow. Hence their mobilization of national man power and energy for the task of building up a sound and stable economy.

How far have they succeeded? Eight years ago in Chungking I witnessed some of the more crazy oscillations of the yuan. It described more dips and curves within a day than a scenic railway within a mile. At the airport and in the Press Hostel minor Kuomintang officials were wont to inquire blandly what currency they might change for you on the black market.

Things have visibly altered in Mao's China, and my own observations were fortified by the comments of long-time foreign residents, more particularly of British businessmen in Shanghai. Despite their grievances—which were many—the old China hands agreed that the Communist government had substantially controlled inflation and put currency on a stable basis. When we were in Shanghai (June, 1952) the prices of sugar and textiles were lower than they had been for many months. Prices of food grains were somewhat higher; but the farmers were getting better returns, and the prices showed no violent fluctuations.

A new unit of value known as the Parity Deposit Unit (P.D.U.) was the main weapon against inflation. It was linked with the four primary necessities—rice, cotton cloth, coal, and edible oil— and it reflected the daily average price of these commodities. By promising the depositor that his money on withdrawal would have the same unit value in terms of these essential goods the Communists encouraged monetary investment and simultaneously reduced the spiral of inflation.

"The new regime," said a Chinese scientist, "does not signify a mere dynastic change. Things have visibly improved. In the old Kuomintang days the currency fluctuated almost from minute to minute. There was no security for anybody—least of all for people like myself. Everybody wanted to be rich quickly. Now things are different. Prices are generally stable. And the majority are happy."

Obviously P.D.U. alone could not have worked the miracle. The principle underlying this system is by no means new to China nor indeed to the world at large for the method of equating money values with staples is no novel expedient. Some say that the savings-unit plan was actually urged by an economist in Kuomintang China whom the authorities ignored. In China rice prices have traditionally been the yardstick for wages and commodity rates. Communist resourcefulness extended the basis to three more basic commodities and thereby helped to cushion conflicting impacts.

Salaries are now paid on a P.D.U. equivalent though in the remote rural regions wages were often quoted to us in terms of catties of rice. The system has undoubtedly made for stability and is a major factor in controlling exchange fluctuations. The "unit price" is published daily in the newspapers and fluctuates very little. But without a simultaneous war against speculation and black-marketing the system's success was doubtful. By forbidding speculation and striking ruthlessly at those who violated the financial regulations the government was able to hold the economic ring and whip the *jen min piao*, or people's notes, into line. Wisely also the Communists have been careful to fix the official rate for foreign currencies at a fair and realistic level.

These measures imply a sufficiency of essential goods throughout the greater part of the country. This explains the government's feverish effort to open out internal communications, intensified by the earlier blockade of the Chinese Nationalists and by the later erection of a *cordon sanitaire* by the Western Powers.

China's rail network extended some 12,500 miles before the war. Of this a fair proportion was damaged or destroyed; moreover nearly a half of the mileage was concentrated in Manchuria. The whole roughly represented a twentieth of the United States' rail network. China has a population thrice that of the United States and an area one and one-third times as large. At a conservative estimate the country needs at least 120,000 railroad miles.

The Communists have made and are making strenuous efforts to remedy this lacuna. Lack of good roads and shipping accentuates their anxiety. Against the 400,000 tons of Kuomintang merchant shipping it is doubtful if the Communists possess 40,000. Although many of the ruined river ports have been rehabilitated, mobility is slow. For river and coastal traffic the Reds lean largely on foreign cargo boats, which are mainly British.

Herculean efforts are under way to reopen, extend, and refurbish the railway services. Very early the Communists succeeded in reopening an old line from the Hwainan coal fields to Yuchikow on the Yangtze and on to Shanghai. Between June, 1950, and the end of 1951 a 280-mile stretch of railway was laid from Chungking to Chengtu. Army personnel aided by nearly 100,000 volunteers helped to open this valuable communication line over the mountains and across the rivers of Szechuan. "Help-Build-the-Railway Committees" were organised, and at Lung-chang the workers tunnelled through more than 800 yards of granite rock under the exotically named Melon Seed cliff.

Here again China seeks to offset lack of equipment and materials by sheer weight of man power. For the most part rail-line construction is concentrated in the southwest and northwest sectors of the country. Aside from the Chungking-Chengtu line the Lunghai railway has been extended from Tienshui some 230 miles to Lanchow, chief city of China's great Northwest. This line constitutes the main lateral trunk railway of the country running along the spine of the six provinces of Shantung, Kiangsu, Anhwei, Honan, Shensi, and Kansu. As in the Southwest, the terrain offered great difficulties, and tunnels frequently caved in through loose soil. The Chinese claim that the workers, by devising a special type of reinforcement, solved a problem which had baffled the foreign-trained experts. Hearing them, I was reminded of Chien Chen-ying's description of the most exciting experience of her life.

"All difficulties," she had remarked, "can be overcome by combining the expert's knowledge with the wisdom and energy of the people."

Apart from occasional forays into the countryside from Peking, we travelled by train continuously for quite nine days. The forays took us to the Great Wall and to Tatung. But, leaving Peking finally, we moved north by rail through Jehol to Mukden across the flat Manchurian plain which spread like a murky carpet around us. Here and there the green sward was clouded by swirling sand and dust.

From Mukden our itinerary ran to Tientsin, where we halted for a day, and then through the verdant loveliness of China's silk

garden of Shantung to Yenchow and Kü-fow; on to Pengpu on
the Hwai River and to Nanking, where the train was ferried over
the Yangtze in three sections. Earlier, on the way from Tientsin
through Shantung, we had crossed the broad, flowing, majestic
Yellow River. From Nanking we turned towards the sea, and our
rail odyssey ended at Shanghai.

We travelled throughout in great comfort. Five bogies, or
coaches, were placed at our disposal—two sleepers for the delegation, another sleeper for the Chinese staff who accompanied us,
a dining car, and an observation car. These coaches were hitched
to one train after another.

Our nine days' journey in an arc running from Mukden
through Tientsin to Shanghai gave us interesting opportunities
for studying the countryside and people. The railways, which
are largely a French legacy, are well maintained. Our own coaches
had the plush ease of continental *wagons-lits;* but the ordinary
coaches occupied by Chinese civilians and soldiers were also
compact and tidy, if strictly utilitarian. On certain trains separate compartments were reserved for women and children. Travel
being restricted in China, the number of passengers nowhere
seemed excessive; and at every station orderly queues with
women and children invariably standing at the head waited for
the train. At nearly every stop loud-speakers blared forth music
and propaganda.

Punctuality is a totalitarian virtue. Like Mussolini's trains
Mao's run on time. You could set your watch by a Chinese train—
certainly by those we travelled in. As in Germany, railway
officials often stand at attention on the platform as a train moves
out. It all seemed very orderly and organised.

Our Chinese companions observed us closely. We were impressed with what we saw; but whether rail communications
could expand at quite the rate the Chinese visualised teased our
minds. By all accounts their rolling stock was limited, and much
of it in poor condition. Of Russian coaches I saw only one,
around two o'clock in the morning as we were approaching

Nanking. Some distance before the ferry on the Yangtze, our train stopped for a few moments; and, coming out on the platform of the observation car, I saw a goods train with sealed-in coaches covered with Russian lettering. They were of a large, different pattern from any I had seen and, unlike the normal green coaches, of a dull brown hue.

Have the Chinese sufficient steel to lay down the many hundreds of new rail miles they visualise? In 1937 the country's production of steel was a little more than 100,000 tons, and its coal output was small even compared with that of Japan, a notoriously poor fuel producer. One estimate placed the 1937 coal figure at one-seventh of Japan's and one-fortieth of that of the United States. The Chinese more than most people can operate on a shoestring; but even the Marxist juggler, known for his sleight of hand, cannot conjure up something out of nothing.

China's rulers appreciate the close link between communications and commerce. They realise that better internal communications mean a quicker flow of trade between town and country, with farmers able to sell their increasing produce more profitably and urban centres better situated to dispose of consumer goods, agricultural implements, and fertilizers to the villages. In other words, better communications spell larger markets for producers and more goods for the people. Along with economic measures, freer rail, road, and water transport helps to stabilise prices, prevent shortages, keep industries supplied with raw materials and consumers with finished goods.

We travelled little by road, apart from driving in and a few miles around various urban centres. Such roads as we used were good to fairish; but from our train it was possible to see and assess the generally dilapidated condition of rural highways. According to Chang Po-chun, Minister of Communications, the Kuomintang troops disrupted some 34,000 miles of highways and destroyed numerous bridges. The Communists say that much of this damage has been repaired, and that Soviet road-building methods, such as the use of the "flexible pavement" theory of the Russian engineer Ivanov, have expedited progress. They point to a new seven-arch 160-yard reinforced concrete bridge in East China as another effort inspired by the Soviet model. Apparently Russian methods of road maintenance are also finding favour in China. Because road transport is as vital for defence as for trade, soldiers and civilians are urged to toil side by side in the work of reconstruction.

Shipping, particularly along the coast and river routes, has come in for special attention. On the Communists' own admission, the Kuomintang removed 56 per cent of the country's steam tonnage, and inflicted heavy damage on wharves, warehouses, and navigation aids. The Reds say they have very largely made good these losses. In June, 1952, Chang Po-chun stated that coastal shipping routes totalling 4,000 nautical miles had been reopened to traffic, while inland water routes were improved and extended to a length of 35,340 miles.

Communist statistics are rarely based on absolute figures; generally they are given in percentages. Thus Chang Po-chun in the same month declared that the total tonnage of publicly and privately owned shipping in China was 39 per cent greater than at the time of the "liberation." "Taking 1950 as 100," he wrote, "the index for freight carried in 1951 was 196. In 1952 it is to be raised further to 267." Chang cited specific instances of how shipping had helped industry. He recalled how, shortly after the Communist capture of Shanghai, Chinese ships had rushed large quantities of North China coal to that city in order to set its industries going again. In 1950 Chinese ships had carried rice down the Yangtze from the southwest provinces to feed the peasants working on the Hwai River and Yellow River projects.

Shortage of river craft and wharf facilities has to some extent been neutralised by the government's expropriatory tactics. In 1951, following the requisitioning by the British authorities in Hongkong of the Chinese tanker *Yung Hao*, the Communists requisitioned the Shell Company's assets throughout China. These included extensive installations, river craft, and other properties.

In 1952 similar retaliatory action followed the handing over by the British authorities at Hongkong of aircraft to an American company. The company, Civil Air Transport Incorporated, had successfully appealed to the Privy Council in London against the decision of the Supreme Court of Hongkong which had originally awarded the planes to the Peking government. In reprisal the Communists requisitioned the two chief British-owned dockyards in Shanghai—Shanghai Dockyards, Limited, and Mollers Shipbuilding & Engineering Works, Limited. At the time of the reprisal Shanghai Dockyards had four dry docks accommodating ships of more than 500 feet and several shipways. Mollers owned large wharf space, shipways, and workshops. In Britain the assets of the two companies were valued at over $8,400,000. Other British firms have let surplus warehouses and factory space to various Chinese government organisations at rentals described by the Hongkong correspondent of *The Times,* London, as "from poor to reasonable."

Even so, it is doubtful if the deficiency has been liquidated. A British businessman in Shanghai, paying a tribute to Chinese resourcefulness, remarked to me that they had good technicians in textile machinery who could turn out most spare parts. Whether they can effectively rebuild the locomotive workshops, repair boilers, and devise spare precision parts is less certain. Almost 80 per cent of China's industrial production is still geared to a pre-machine-age level. But the Communists are learning fast.

In the early days they made mistakes. They still do; but most of the old China hands I met agreed that their mistakes were progressively fewer.

"The difficulty with the Communists," said a British businessman in Shanghai, "is not their commercial morality. That's extraordinarily high. I've only known of two instances where the government has gone back on its undertaking. The trouble with them is that they have too many amateurs in business. They sometimes don't understand."

This was said in June, 1952, at the end of the San Fan movement when the national bourgeoisie, or capitalists, indigenous and foreign, found themselves isolated from one another and from the government. Although the movement was initially directed against the corrupt commercial elements, many foreign businessmen felt that it had developed into a large-scale purge of the commercial community, with the masses "let loose on a long leash." In their opinion, it was a war in which the people were associated with the government against "the common enemy." It was a class war led by the working class. Its aim was the terrorisation and ultimate elimination of the bourgeoisie.

At some stage the Communists appear to have realised that they were going too far. In June, 1950, Mao Tse-tung, after unleashing an indiscriminate liquidation campaign against the landlords and rich peasants, had called for a change in the Communist attitude to the rich peasant. "We must preserve our rich peasant economy," he had warned, "for nothing matters so much as the restoration of production in the rural areas."

Almost exactly two years later the Communist regime seems to have been afflicted by the same doubts and hesitations *vis-à-vis* the national bourgeoisie. China's prime priority is higher production. The ruthless prosecution of the San Fan and Wu Fan movements was threatening to kill the capitalist goose which laid the golden eggs. The Communists were seized with second thoughts. In the latter half of 1952 they beat a strategic retreat— how strategic, was revealed by W. C. Gomersall, director of China Engineers, Limited, and chairman of Shanghai Worsted Mills, to the Hongkong correspondent of *The Times*, London, who interviewed him in November, 1952. Mr. Gomersall is reported as saying that the anticorruption campaign had produced complete economic paralysis and had damaged industrial relations but the authorities had attained their objectives in removing irregularities, and when the campaign closed they had fostered improved relations. "Industrial relations were now better than they had ever been, with increased production as the major incentive." *

* *The Times*, London, Nov. 25, 1952.

Increased production is the key to the Communists' economic programme. Most other considerations are subordinate to it. To ensure greater agricultural output the Communists have shown themselves willing to tolerate the rich peasants and even those landlords who use their land directly for industrial and commercial purposes. For the same reason they allow the small trader and capitalist to operate in the business field.

With the shrinking of foreign trade the Red regime draws more heavily on its internal resources, and concentrates on developing them. It has come to believe that through rural progress lies the way to industrial development. Although the Chinese speak a great deal about industrial reconstruction, I have a feeling that their immediate attention is devoted to agriculture. Land reforms, they reckon, by increasing the output of the soil will raise the peasants' purchasing power and create new and larger demands for more implements and fertilizers and for improved techniques. In turn this must stimulate urban production, and China ultimately will emerge as a strong industrial State with no vestige of foreign capitalism.

Admittedly this is not so simple as it sounds. And the Communists are aware of it. Wholesale expropriation of land and parcelling out of it among the peasants would have meant uneconomic and possibly decreased cultivation. For this reason the Communists, while redistributing the land, have been careful to protect the rich peasant and the industrial landlord. Despite these precautions pressure on the land must increase with growing population. It is a truism that the first fruits of industrialisation are more mouths to feed. India and Japan provide the classic examples. In China the simultaneous Communist drive to improve living conditions for the masses and to enforce better hygiene, public health, and sanitation furnishes a further stimulus to the growth of population. Whether the production curve can keep ahead of the population curve has still to be determined.

The Communists do not appear to be unduly disturbed by this cycle. Trained to think of production in terms of man power, they are sceptical of the Western view that a rise in population must automatically eat into the new wealth of industrialisation. They prefer to think that in the long term increased man power means increased production. Meanwhile the introduction of the Stakhanovite principle in field and factory with its glorification of Labour Heroes and Heroines provides a major stimulus.

China has many obstacles to overcome in achieving her industrial nirvana. Apart from lack of equipment, she suffers from an acute deficiency of trained scientists, technicians, and skilled workers as well as doctors, nurses, and teachers. The expedited courses for turning out such personnel have partially repaired the deficiency, but it is still very considerable. Even enthusiasm cannot cover a multitude of lacks.

It is possible, however, to exaggerate the difficulties and to indulge in dangerously wishful thinking. China's industrial potential is impressive, and she has considerable resources in tungsten, gypsum, antimony, tin, asbestos, mica, graphite, fluorite, and sulphur. She has also some coal and iron ore; but these deposits are comparatively small and badly sited in relation to each other, except in Manchuria. Conceit is the rock on which Communism in China might founder; but with intellectual arrogance the Reds combine a confidence tinged with unusually sober realism. Mao's men have not run amuck like the Russian Bolsheviks of early days.

The Chinese talent for improvisation has helped solve some minor problems, though Communist propagandists often tend to magnify the achievements beyond reasonable bounds. Devices making for technical improvement and the elimination of wastage are encouraged and popularised, and movements such as the Red Banner Production Competition, the Patriotic Productive Emulation Drive, the Shock-Workers' Movement, and the Movement for Increased Production and Economy seek to mobilise and canalise the workers' initiative and energy in productive channels. A prominent Labour Heroine is the eighteen-year-old girl spinner Ho Chien-hsiu, whose working technique has reduced waste and made her nationally famous. If all textile mills in China could reduce their percentage of waste to her rate of 0.25 per cent the country, according to the Communists, would annually gain an additional 45,000 bales of yarn without any increase of machinery, man power, or raw material consumption. Moreover they calculate that the cloth woven from this extra yarn would meet the annual requirements of four million people.

Zeal at times outruns discretion. The utilitarian motif initially led the Communists to such exaggerated gestures as the encouragement of soap manufacture instead of the fine porcelains, pewters, and curios turned out in Peking's famous Street of the Antiquaries. Incense manufacturers were called upon to produce matches, and a shop dealing in mirrors was required to sell shoes. The balance is being righted, though even today household goods occasionally jostle a Tang horse and domestic articles flank a Ming vase or a Han bronze.

The difficulty of knowing where to draw the line is another totalitarian ailment. When the Communists seized power they were realistic enough to acknowledge that the country's spindles would not whirl without substantial imports of raw cotton. They accordingly set about procuring them. Unfortunately the Chinese Nationalists' blockade compelled shippers to land the cotton in places as far removed as Hongkong, Tientsin, and Tsingtao and from there, after long waits in godowns, the cotton was carried by rail to Shanghai. This added considerably to the bill of costs.

In an effort to reduce raw cotton imports the Communists launched a drive for improving and accelerating the transport of indigenous cotton, and cultivation also was encouraged. In 1950 it was planned to make China self-sufficient in this commodity within three years. The campaign met with fair success, but the Communists overlooked one small point. In their zeal to carry self-sufficiency a step further they forbade the import of wool tops and ordered substitution by Chinese wool. It was soon discovered that factories which had turned to Chinese wool were unable to sell their products because of their poor and crude quality. Realistically, if belatedly, the Communists resumed the import of wool tops.

In Mukden, as also in Shanghai, I had occasion to visit some industrial plants. My earlier visits to technical and scientific institutes had led me to suspect that the Chinese were in no position to launch large-scale industrial production without two prerequisites. These were foreign technical assistance and a reservoir of technical talent. What I saw of their industrial plants largely reinforced this view.

Few Asian countries are more adept at window-dressing their wares. In Canton I saw a Products Exhibition which gave me my first glimpse of Communist propaganda on the economic front. Charts and diagrams were effectively designed and displayed. On the wall of one pavilion was a fair-sized poster showing a factory owner bound in ropes and standing abjectly before a mob of howling workers. Elsewhere were pictures of Labour Heroes and Heroines.

The Mukden Industrial Exhibition was a more impressive affair. It included sections devoted to steel and iron, textile manufactures, cement, soap, asbestos, and shale products. Even my scientific colleague, the mildly cynical Dr. Bhagavantam, was impressed. But he remained sceptical.

"I can't understand it," he remarked as we walked out. "Did you see that high-precision lathe on the ten-foot bed? And the high-powered motors, turbines, and generators? We manufacture none of these in India. To produce them on a commercial scale the Chinese would need hundreds of trained technicians in the lower grades. Where are they?"

We entered into a pretty arithmetical calculation on the basis of what we had seen at Tsinghua University in Peking, which is China's chief technical training centre.

"Let's sort it out," said Bhagavantam. "This year at Tsinghua they have 3,000 students. Since the course takes four years some 700 graduates must be graduated every year. But the People's

Republic was proclaimed only in 1949. Therefore the first trained batch should be turned out only in 1953."

I remarked on the possibilities of their expedited courses, but Bhagavantam shook his head doubtfully.

"If this is the industrial progress they've made," he went on, "it's incredible. They produce more varieties of steel than we do— soft, magnetic, and high-precision tool steel. Also hard steel. Of course, the guide was talking nonsense when he said it was eight point. Diamond is ten. What I'd like to see is a large-scale factory of theirs with an assembly line."

We saw one very soon—a machine-tool factory at Mukden. On going around we discovered that all it produced was a five-foot ordinary lathe and a cutter machine. The head of the factory was not a technician but a party man. He was evasive about the output. The factory was originally built by the Japanese, and its capital equipment was largely Japanese supplemented by some Russian machinery. Coming to the assembly line, we saw about a dozen each of the five-foot lathes and cutter machines. The major resources of the factory were engaged in turning out spare parts of these two models.

A much-bemedalled Labour Hero showed us around.

"Was a great deal of damage done to the factory during the war?" I asked, mindful of the Soviet denudations.

"Yes," assented the Labour Hero eagerly. "The Japanese did much damage before they surrendered. And after that the Kuomintang destroyed a great deal."

It was then that we saw them. In a corner of the assembly hall stood two high-precision lathes on ten-foot beds, and they were the exact prototypes of the one we had seen at the Industrial Exhibition. There was one difference. The exhibit had Chinese markings. These two had unconcealed Russian letterings. Bhagavantam glanced at me and smiled.

"One of two things has happened," he said later. "Either the exhibit we saw was assembled here from parts imported from

Russia; or it is possible that Russian technicians with Chinese aid and indigenous material manufactured one or two of these here as exhibits. I can't believe that they are being turned out on a large scale."

Near Mukden we also visited a coal mine and a shale-oil plant. The coal mine, known as Lung Men, was in the eastern sector of the city of Fushun. It was one of several in the area and produced a superior type of coal used for tempering steel. Here again we heard the story of Japanese and Kuomintang destruction. We could obtain no absolute figures or statistics. Production, we were told, had gone up 4.6 times as compared with 1949. Wages were twice as high. By some questioning we learned that the average wage for a skilled workman, presumably of the foreman grade, was approximately $50 a month reckoned in terms of P.D.U.

We saw the workmen's dormitories, with four unmarried men sharing a room and separate quarters for the married men. They were reasonably comfortable and clean. Near by were a rest house and a sanatorium where workers convalescing from illness could stay for a month. They paid a third of the cost of their food; the rest was borne by the State.

In the afternoon we visited an open coal pit under the lazy sunshine. The coal here was of ordinary fuel quality, but the seams were from 260 to 280 feet long and made a pretty pattern with layers of green, brown, black, and grey. Bhagavantam thought that there was pyrite intermixed with the shale and coal.

Later in the same day we went around a shale-oil refinery. Shale and its products had figured prominently at the Mukden Industrial Exhibition. This plant had been put up in 1928, and much of the machinery was Japanese. It was not unimpressive. From shale they were extracting crude oil and lubricating oil, kerosene and petroleum. A by-product was paraffin wax, and Bhagavantam was particularly interested to see that sulphur was being extracted from iron sulphide. But once again no absolute production figures were available.

The dyeing and printing factory that we saw in Shanghai had

been built by the Japanese in 1931. Before leaving for it we received sample books of colourful prints; but in the factory itself the print varieties were restricted to a very few. Production was mainly concentrated on blue cotton cloth for the regulation uniform suits now favoured by the mass of Chinese. The machinery was Japanese. We were told of the workers' patriotism and initiative, which had led them to suggest rationalisation schemes to increase output and effect economies. Wages had increased, and improved safety devices spoke of the State's solicitude for the workers.

Looking back, I feel that he who would dogmatise on China's economic situations is a rash man. Lack of reliable and comprehensive statistics induces caution, and personal observation is circumscribed by many limiting factors. For the most part we saw what our hosts wished us to see; and it would be legitimate to assume that the things shown were calculated to impress. If all of them did not, it is because unintelligent propaganda led some of us to expect more in certain departments than we actually observed. Judgment cannot be dogmatic, and the objective observer can only cite the facts as he saw them for the record.

What backing China's currency has—some say it is commodities—and what motivations influence Marxist finance are known only to Peking's financial pundits such as Po Yi-po, the Finance Minister, and Nan Han-chen, head of the People's Bank. Neither is overexpansive. Undoubtedly the Western blockade is driving China deeper into the economic orbit of Russia and Eastern Europe. The Moscow Economic Conference of 1952 sought to by-pass the blockade by cutting across intermediaries and businessmen and dealing directly with manufacturers. "The Moscow conference," confessed Nan Han-chen, "was called to render useless the blockade so that all countries could trade for the benefit of all. China has been trading on a cash basis for a long time. But for the blockade we would not have instituted barter."

China's Communists are not averse to taxation, even of the peasants, nor to profit for the capitalist. In Communist as in democratic countries taxation has a dual object—to produce revenue and to curb inflation.

Even when confined to the loess hills of Yenan the Communists had levied taxation on a scale progressing from a floor of 3 per cent to a ceiling of 35 per cent. Imposts were collected in tax and grain. In 1943 the peasants paid a grain levy of roughly 30 per cent of their produce in a normal year. Today the figure appears to be between 18 and 27 per cent.

On the plea that in the long years preceding "liberation" the peasants had borne the brunt of national taxation while the urban classes had waxed rich by a combination of corruption, profiteering, and tax dodging the Communist regime bore down heavily on these elements. In June, 1952, a British businessman in Shanghai explained to me the division of taxation and profit, saying the Chinese businessman paid taxes on gross turnover rather than on net profits. Having done this, he was theoretically allowed around 15 per cent of the profit. Of the remainder he had to put aside not less than 10 per cent as reserves, 8 per cent as dividend, 60 per cent for bonuses to shareholders and 7 per cent for social welfare. The range and impact of taxation have oscillated with the government's needs. Like all totalitarian administrations, the Communist regime prefers to deal with large units; and it has been known to levy taxation on a particular industry, say textiles, on a blanket basis, leaving each firm or factory to determine its individual contribution to the collective quota. This obviates the need for a top-heavy tax-collecting machinery and throws the onus for payment on the industry as a whole.

Recently the administration has tended to levy arbitrary imposts on foreign firms. In November, 1952, a British businessman complained that the government's tax bureau had assessed his company's profits at three times the amount shown in the balance sheet. Simultaneously the bureau had placed its own unilateral value on stocks. The company had thereby been required to pay in income tax a sum greater than its total profits; and in order to do this it had had to remit nearly 1,700,000 Hongkong dollars from its Hongkong funds. In October, 1952, the tax bureau had called on it for an advance payment of income tax for 1952; and after vain protests it had to give up nearly 800,000 Hongkong dollars which the bureau remarked it might recover when the books for 1952 were closed. Various intermediate imposts, such as commodity taxes and business turnover taxes, are levied also. In the textile industry the former averaged some 16 per cent of the manufacturing cost of cloth.

In the Kuomintang days British banks and business houses used to advance money to Chinese businessmen at 7 to 8 per cent with a fairly generous margin of time for repayment. The Government Bank at that time charged 12 to 13 per cent. Today the Chinese banks under Communist aegis have steadily dropped the interest rate for loans; but these are not normally available to private industry.

Many believe that unemployment is unknown in a Communist El Dorado. In China the regime has frankly confessed the existence of 3,000,000 unemployed. Unemployment touches all strata of society, including the capitalists hit by the Wu Fan movement, the small traders squeezed out by the expanding activities of the Mao Yi Kung Ssu (the State trading company, which apart from buying rural produce sponsors retail shops in the towns), and peasant families—who, lacking full-time occupation on their modest holdings, are underemployed. Moreover even urban wages are often insufficient for maintaining a family. This partly explains the Communist drive to attract women to the armed services and to work as parachutists, postmen, engineers, and transport drivers. Former Kuomintang officers and officials who have emerged purified from the ordeal of the "people's supervision" also require rehabilitation. Among the unemployed are a number of intellectuals.

The budget of the Central People's Government is more difficult than most to decipher and unravel. In August, 1952, the 1952 budget was adopted by the Central People's Government Council and officially described as "the first budget in China's history planned to balance." It registered an increase of 41.66 per cent over the previous year's budget and a rise of 55.52 per cent in expenditure. The Finance Minister, Po Yi-po, stated that in 1951 the total output of agriculture "was restored to 92.8 per cent of the highest prewar annual level" while in 1952 the total production of grain was "expected to exceed the highest level in the history of China." Industrial output in 1951 was 26.7 per cent more than in the previous year, and "a still bigger increase" was promised in 1952. Acknowledgment was made to "the selfless help of the U.S.S.R."

In 1950 urban taxes headed all sources of revenue, with agricultural tax second and profits from State enterprises third. In 1951 urban taxes were followed by profits from State enterprises, with agricultural tax third. In 1952 the returns from State enterprise constituted the largest single item of revenue. The Communists say that the load is being lifted from the backs of the long-suffering peasantry. That, if true, is thought-provoking.

From a seemingly haphazard jumble of acts and policies a pattern of economic living is slowly emerging. The pieces of this complicated jigsaw puzzle are falling into place. On the economic as on the political plane authority is being centralised in a number of organisations which will operate under the all-seeing eye of Peking. The strings are being gathered and pulled together by one controlling hand.

In June, 1952, as the San Fan and Wu Fan movements drew to a close, the formation of the All-China Confederation of Industry and Commerce was announced. Through this body the Central Government obviously plans to control private industrialists and traders who have survived the anticorruption blizzard. Much the same motivations inspire the new agricultural tax regulations, also announced in June, 1952, which base taxes on production quotas and thereby make possible an over-all control over the farmers. The establishment of security organs in every village office and factory completes this process.

In April, 1952, a readjustment of China's university system

was announced whereby technical instruction was to be centralised. This falls into the general pattern, because its evident aim is to step up efficiency and thereby stimulate the nation's economic programme. Even the unemployment regulations, promulgated in August, 1952, seem designed to control labour. They differentiate among the three major groups likely to be unemployed—the town labourers, the rural peasants, and the intellectuals. Surplus man power is to be utilised to develop all-round efficiency. A similar regimentation inspires the general programme for implementing regional autonomy for the national minorities which Peking also announced in August. "Under the unified economic system and economic construction plan of the State," declares Article 20, "all autonomous organs shall freely develop local autonomy."

Thus the network of central control spreads over every phase of the country's economic life, reaching into the farthest crannies and corners of Mao's China.

11

AS MAO DECREES

India has a saying that goes back to Mogul days: "Delhi dur ast"—"Delhi is far away." China has a not dissimilar proverb: "Heaven is high and the Emperor is far away." In ancient China and India the government was a remote entity. To some extent the feeling persists in India; but it does not prevail in China. There is no sphere of life, private or public, into which Mao's government does not intrude. As Dr. Hu Shih remarked in another context: "The individual is denied even his right of silence."

In democratic countries individual rights are defined under two heads: rights *in rem* and rights *in personam*, which might roughly be defined as property and personal rights. In China the individual's contractual rights are limited to his relations with the State, and the State predominates over the individual. The community or State, not the individual, counts.

One of the first acts of the Communist rulers was to scrap the laws of the previous regime, so that the civil and criminal laws compiled by the Kuomintang lost force. As a result there is little or no formal law in the country today. So far as I could ascertain, the only laws to be codified are those relating to marriage, trade unions, and land. For the rest, and until such time as a comprehensive legal code is compiled, the Common Programme adopted by the Chinese People's Political Consultative Conference in the fall of 1949 provides the chief basis of law.

The Common Programme, which might loosely be defined as China's temporary constitution, has four parts. The first part enunciates the principles governing the people's democratic dictatorship and contains sixty articles. The second and third parts define the organic law respectively of the Chinese People's Political Consultative Conference and the Central People's Government. The last part contains the Declaration of the first plenary session of the C.P.P.C.C. "All laws, decrees, and judicial systems of the Kuomintang reactionary government which oppress the people shall be abolished," declares Article 17. "Laws and decrees protecting the people shall be enacted, and the people's judicial system shall be established."

The Marriage Law was promulgated by the Central People's Government on May 1, 1950. In the following month the government simultaneously enacted the Trade Union Law and the Agrarian Reform Law.

Justice in China is dispensed at the highest level by the Supreme People's Court, which directs and supervises the work of all judicial bodies of the country and consists of a Chief Justice or President, two Vice-Presidents, and fourteen committee members. Below this court are People's Courts at provincial, county, district, and subdistrict levels. Not all the judges of these courts are trained lawyers. Indeed the majority would appear to have been chosen more for political reliability and "understanding of the masses" than for knowledge of law. A veteran nonparty jurist, Shen Chun-ju, is President of the Supreme People's Court, content to dispense the law as the Communists ordain it; but we were a little taken aback to discover that the Chief Judge of the People's Court at Tientsin, a devout party member, had no legal training whatsoever. This seemed to be the rule rather than the exception. The judges of the Supreme People's Court are today the nominees of the Central Government while those at the lower level are appointed by the people's local conference or assembly. Later it is planned to elect all of them.

That legal knowledge and training are not regarded as essential prerequisites for judgeship is perhaps not surprising in a system which has little use for lawyers and even less for formal law. Apart from the three enactments relating to agrarian reform, marriage, and trade unionism, only a few decrees have been formulated on the basis of the experience of the past four years. Thus the February trial held in Peking in 1952 at the height of the San Fan and Wu Fan movements has led to the promulgation of a number of maxims and decrees, the majority being of a prohibitory character.

Modern China knows no case law. This is a departure from Kuomintang practice, which drew heavily on American and British legal precedents.

"The law of new China does not call for elaborate interpretation," remarked Shen Chun-ju. "Hence we have no need for legal experts and specialists. Ours is a law which the ordinary man can understand. The dictum of Chairman Mao that 'conclusions should only be reached after thorough analysis and investigation' is enough for our purpose. It is the guiding dictum of the People's Courts throughout China."

We visited a People's Court in Peking and another in Shanghai. Two divorce applications were disposed of by the Peking tribunal. At the Shanghai court a murder trial was in progress.

The accused was a hard-faced, stolid woman who was charged with killing her maidservant some ten years earlier. It was "a preliberation murder" as our interpreter described it. The three judges were men, and alongside them sat a member of the All-China Democratic Women's Federation. In the new China a People's Representative, who is generally a member of the accused's trade union, sits in court with the judges and appears to combine the functions of jury and counsel.

The accused had her own lawyer, but he took no part in the proceedings while we were there. In fact he sat on the bench with us, and we should have taken him for a spectator if our interpreter had not identified him.

The courtroom was packed. The accused woman stood in the well of the court with two armed policemen behind her.

"She is known as the Tigress of Shanghai," said our interpreter.

The case had evidently excited considerable interest. We were provided with copies of the charge sheet, according to which the woman had consistently ill-treated her twelve-year-old maid-servant and had finally set her on fire. When the maidservant died the neighbours had complained to the police, charging the woman with murder. But the Kuomintang police had been bribed, and no case was lodged against her. On the contrary, the complainants were warned "not to make trouble."

The accused admitted the crime, pleading only that the maid-servant was lazy; but she strenuously denied that she had bribed the Kuomintang police. The questioning was done entirely by the judges and did not extend over half an hour.

Various witnesses, including the woman's sister-in-law, testified against her. These also were questioned exclusively by the judges, and neither the accused nor her counsel asked them any questions. At the end of each witness's examination, the judges cross-examined the accused. There appeared to be no rules of evidence or procedure, and the proceedings were informal to a degree. But they certainly were expeditious: four witnesses were disposed of within a half-hour.

We did not wait for the conclusion of the trial.

"She will die," said our interpreter conclusively.

The evidence presented pointed to the woman's guilt, and I am prepared to believe that she was guilty of the crime charged. But two items on the charge sheet intrigued me and threw a revealing light on the motivations of Communist justice.

Item One recounted that the woman's husband, who was dead, had been "an Imperialist stooge." Apparently he had worked as a foreman in a British factory and had been done to death by his infuriated fellow workers during a strike. Item Two related to the woman's son, who was also dead. He, the charge sheet alleged, had been in league with the Japanese military police during the occupation.

It is possible that both characterisations were true. But what had they to do with the guilt or innocence of the accused on a murder charge? In Communist jurisprudence they obviously count.

China's new legal system makes lawyers redundant. Old-time legal practitioners have been forced to find employment in other fields, though their services may occasionally be requisitioned. Very rarely the State may cite them as expert legal witnesses. Occasionally a party to a suit may request the government for permission to employ a lawyer. Alternatively he may do so on his own initiative, but here there is one significant proviso. The lawyer employed must be a member of a "progressive" party. In none of these cases is a lawyer paid. Nor are there court fees. Justice in China is certainly economic, and expeditious.

Alongside the Supreme People's Court functions the People's Procurator-General's office. This body is vested with supreme supervisory power "to ensure the strict observance of the law by all government institutions and public functionaries as well as by nationals of the country." At present it consists of a Procurator-General, two deputies, and eleven committee members. Shen Chun-ju, President of the Supreme People's Court, is not a member of the party. But Lo Jung-huan, the Procurator-General, is very much the party man. He is a member of the Communist Central Committee or Politburo.

The vast majority, if not all, of the more important trials originate in the office of the Procurator-General, who may initiate investigations on complaint or suspicion. If a *prima facie* case is established the accused may be called upon to confess his guilt. In nine cases out of ten he does, and the mills of Communist justice then grind swiftly.

The dispensation of law, like every other activity in China, is governed by the Communist credo. Politics predominate. In

China there is no rule of law as democratic countries understand it. The judiciary is the instrument of the executive and has no being apart from it. The President of the People's Supreme Court is also a member of the government. While we were in Peking he went to Manchuria on a political mission concerned with the national minorities. Thus the law is governed by politics, which in turn is influenced by the economic structure. In this sense justice is on a par with politics and economics.

Much is made of the fact that the old Kuomintang laws were static and not abreast of contemporary social needs and developments. The Communist laws, it is claimed, are flexible and related to the people's interests. That may be; but, where the State dominates, this only means that the law can be adjusted to suit the whims of the totalitarian rulers.

China, like other police States, ignores where it does not suppress the liberty of the individual. Of President Roosevelt's Four Freedoms, freedom from want is assured though not always achieved, and so theoretically is freedom of religion though the foreign missionary has been hounded out of the country. Freedom from fear is conspicuous by its absence, and despite Article 5 of the Common Programme, which guarantees "freedom of thought, speech, publication, assembly, association, correspondence, person, domicile, change of domicile, religious belief and the freedom of holding processions and demonstrations," there is no freedom of expression. As a journalist I was interested to see that the English-language newspaper, the *Shanghai News*, religiously produced almost every day the editorial of the semiofficial *People's Daily* of Peking. It rarely printed its own editorial.

The absence of the rule of law implies the presence of a police State. Despite its verbal trappings this is the character of Mao's China. Freedom of speech, assembly, and association is theoretically guaranteed; but the Communists do not disguise the fact that such freedom can be enjoyed only by "the people." On July 1, 1949, the twenty-eighth anniversary of the founding of the Chinese Communist party, Mao made this demonstrably plain.

" 'You are dictatorial,' " he declared, quoting his opponents. "Yes, dear gentlemen, you are right, and we are really that way. The experiences of several decades amassed by the Chinese people tell us to carry out the people's democratic dictatorship. That is, the right of reactionaries to voice their opinion must be taken away, and only people are to be allowed to have the right of voicing their opinion. Who are the 'people'? At the present stage in China they are the working class, the peasant class, the petty bourgeoisie, and national bourgeoisie. Under the leadership of the working class and the Communist party, these classes unite to form their own State and elect their own government to enact dictatorship over the lackeys of imperialism—the landlord class, the bureaucratic-capitalist class, and the Kuomintang reactionaries and their henchmen." Freedom in Mao's China means freedom only to voice the rulers' opinions.

Article 5 of the Common Programme notwithstanding, there seems to be very little freedom of movement inside the country. Control of residence was known in Kuomintang days. In reimposing it the Communists have made it more stringent. I was told by a foreign diplomat of long standing that after the "liberation" all Chinese nationals inside the country were required to register. The Communists explained that this was done merely for census purposes; but there appear to be more motives for the requirement. Every individual Chinese carries an identity card. According to one European resident, if a Chinese stayed more than two nights at another person's place, he or she had to notify the police. When I inquired of Kung Peng, director of the information department of the Ministry of Foreign Affairs, if that were so she denied it hotly. The over-two-nights report rule, she insisted, applied only to certain foreigners whose movements were restricted.

On the other hand, though freedom of travel exists in theory it is greatly circumscribed in practice. A Chinese buying a railway ticket is generally questioned by the authorities at his place of departure, and he is required to report to the local authorities at his destination. In certain cases, a one-way ticket without return may be issued to him. The extent of surveillance differs from place to place. In the bigger cities and towns the iron hand operates behind a velvet glove; but in outlying rural areas the authoritarian character of the regime is more nakedly evident. I was told that religious toleration ostensibly practised in urban centres was virtually dead in many of the rural districts.

Setting up one class against another, children against parents, and students against teachers is part of the Communist technique. Life is particularly hard for the middle classes, who must now make do on small salaries and, in order to ingratiate themselves with the regime, must rise early every morning to attend indoctrination classes. During our railway journey we saw these early morning classes in session at many stations.

I heard many stories of the authorities' autocratic behaviour, some amusing, some sad. As a rule, a person called upon to "confess" his or her sin is rarely told what it is. A Chinese married woman taken with her husband to a police station was ordered to "confess." Ignorant of the charge, she shamefacedly confessed she had a lover; but that was not the sin the authorities were interested in. It ultimately was revealed that a servant had reported her for listening on the radio to the Voice of America. Meanwhile her married life had been ruined.

It is not unusual for employees to be asked to reveal their employers' sins. During the San Fan movement one official was denounced by his chauffeur for wasting petrol by having his lady friend driven home from a dance club. In Tsingsi county of Kwangsi province seven *kanpus*, or minor officials, were degraded for marrying the daughters of "reactionary, antirevolutionary landlords." Another party official was charged with "dissipation such as building a private garden, going to dancing halls, and lewdly playing with females." This resourceful gentleman was also accused of possessing "a bureaucratic and patriarchal manner."

An Englishwoman in Shanghai whose Chinese chauffeur injured

a pedestrian was hauled to the police station where she was held for five hours and lectured on the iniquitous behaviour of foreigners towards the Chinese people. Throughout this period she was not allowed to telephone home. A British businessman related how pressure was brought on his Chinese executives to join the workers' union. They were subjected to hours of indoctrination and thought reform and finally asked to declare whether they were capitalists or workers. Of course, they said they were workers.

Public confession is now part of the ordained ritual. At the height of the San Fan and Wu Fan movements it took the form of "brain-washing" or "brain-changing," whereby the errant were required to reorientate their individual minds for the greater service of the State. This type of intellectual spring cleaning was particularly popular at the universities, where for quite four months students and professors wallowed in an ideological Turkish bath. "Face" counts for much in the Chinese pattern of social behaviour, and the loss of face involved in public confession and self-criticism suggests a shrewd association of politics with psychology.

Freedom of the press is among the first casualties in a dictatorship. New China's newspapers make dull reading. They are of a uniform pattern, and "news" comprises largely statements and speeches by party leaders with small snippets of foreign happenings supplied generally by the official Hsinhua News Agency which distils the dregs of the Soviet Tass and other Red sources of news, such as *L'Humanité* of Paris. Even the style of writing is stereotyped. The "crimes of the American Imperialists and Kuomintang reactionaries" are prominently featured and denounced. Slogans provide a patterned refrain. The deeds of Labour Heroes and Heroines are eulogised. While we were there, statements and articles on America's alleged bacteriological warfare formed our daily diet. Chinese newspapers carry a few advertisements, but these are generally of cinema and theatre shows and art exhibitions.

A few newspapers are still privately owned, but their publication is rigidly controlled. A newspaper must state the occupation, political opinions, and political affiliations of its editor and publisher. It is also required to disclose its financial position and the source of its income, and before permission for publication is granted it must solemnly undertake not to spread news or propaganda injurious to the regime. It would appear that a form of self-censorship operates in each individual newspaper office where Communist "copy-tasters" ensure that the material published conforms to the regime's requirements. Such self-censorship is the better part of political and journalistic wisdom.

Institutes and organisations are similarly controlled. All societies—social, economic, or educational—must be registered. Like the press, they are required to name their sponsors and give details of their political aims and beliefs, the sources of their funds, and their affiliations with other organisations. Similarly they must pledge themselves not to engage in activities detrimental to the People's Democracy.

More subtle and subterranean tactics have been employed against the academic world, which was long hostile to the Kuomintang regime. Initially the Communists refrained from interfering in the internal affairs of the universities and left these bodies in charge of elected committees of the faculty; but thereafter pressure was applied at various points, and a Red tinge soon coloured the curricula. Marxism, the New Democracy, and the "philosophy of the masses" displaced the older conventional subjects, and Russian is steadily edging out English as a second language.

Heaven, to the Chinese mind, has always been high and remote. As a people the Chinese are more concerned with mundane matters than with the supernatural sanctions of heaven. Like Hinduism, Confucianism is a way of life which does not demand from its followers a belief in God. Just as the Hindu joint family system elevates the collective motif, so Chinese thought over many centuries has inclined to group rather than individual action. The average Chinese is more interested in the family as a whole than in the individuals who compose it, more absorbed in the possibilities of governmental action than in the problems of the individual soul. Being intensely practical, he would understand and appreciate a rigid, certain, immutable orthodoxy. The god which Confucianism failed to provide, Communism strives to give. It would make all men in the image of Marx.

Christianity as a whole, despite missionary claims, appears to have made little impress on the Chinese mind and outlook. There is evidence to suggest that the heterodox Christianity of the Nestorian creed made some headway during the Tang period; but few traces of it remain, and it is possible that the Christianity of the nineteenth century which brought the Bible behind the gunboat has fallen on equally infertile soil. Identified with imperialism, Christianity has also suffered from the contrary claims of Catholic and Protestant missionaries. It seemed to many Chinese as if these were conflicting religions that shared merely a vague loyalty to a common Godhead. The identification of Christianity with the ruling circles of the corrupt Kuomintang depressed its prestige further.

Western thought and learning did not produce the impact on China that it did on India, where it released a ferment of liberal ideas and educated Indians began to talk in the accents of Edmund Burke and John Stuart Mill, of Adam Smith, Darwin and Spencer. Mao had read these writers long before he discovered Marx; but their liberal thought made a much lighter impress on the Chinese mind than on the Indian. To many Chinese, Communism is more easily acceptable than liberalism as a creed because it is nearer to their traditions and thought patterns. The people, like the heaven of old, are supreme. In the old days the Emperor was the representative of heaven. Today the Communist party poses as the hand and voice of the people.

It is against this background that China's present attitude to the foreign missionary must be viewed. If Christianity has made little impress on China on the strictly religious plane, its sense of dedicated social service imported new values which have made their mark. In a sense the Communists, by emulating this spirit, have provided the revolutionary leaven which Christianity failed to give.

Knowing their own countrymen the Communists calculate that Christianity, if divorced from its Western moorings, will perish on Chinese soil. This is the rationale behind their drive against the foreign missionary. By identifying him with the foreign imperialists with whom he long enjoyed extraterritorial rights and the right to acquire property, the regime has found it comparatively easy to canalise and concentrate popular hostility in that direction. If Christianity is to remain in China, the Communists ordain, it must be as a Chinese form of Christianity. Indigenous Catholics must take their spiritual orders from indigenous priests and bishops. There can be no extraterritorial loyalty to the Vatican. In the New Reformed Church the Communists have planted the first seeds of a new Oriental Gallicanism.

It was interesting to compare the impact of Christianity on India with that on China. In India the British, while tacitly encouraging the spread of Christianity, had overtly prevented the foreign missionary from acquiring too much power. Between the British civil servant and the British businessman was a clear division. This extended between businessman and missionary. No such cleavage existed in the old China, where the foreign trader and the foreign missionary often worked hand in hand. In India any wounding of indigenous religious susceptibilities had provoked rebellion. The removal of caste marks led to the Vellore mutiny, and the reported use of pig's grease for cartridges was a prime inflammatory factor in the Great Mutiny of 1857. Less sensitive to indignities against religion, the Chinese were more alive to its political implications. In the old days the Chinese Christians were a privileged class, and it was not uncommon for a magistrate to favour a Christian son or brother in disputes on domestic estates.

The drive against the foreign missionaries is pursued vehemently and with venom. Many of these individuals, the vast majority, have laboured selflessly for the good of the common Chinese, hoping only to garner souls for the Vineyard of the Lord. Incredible tales of missionaries' eating the livers of children and using their eyes for medical purposes were concocted by fanatical rural *kanpus* in a drive to whip up the feeling of ignorant and credulous peasants against them. Many moving stories of missionary forbearance and heroism percolated through the propaganda. Not all the Chinese, even in remote villages, reacted strongly to the *kanpus'* agitation. I was told of a Catholic nun who, on being deported from a Manchurian village, had to travel two days by train to Tientsin. At regular intervals the radio on the train blared forth the news that there was an evil foreign missionary aboard on her way out of China. Yet no one of the scores of Chinese fellow passengers around her touched or reviled her.

The day of the foreign missionary is definitely over in China. Isolated from the West, Chinese Christianity seems doomed to wilt and die. Mao will not have the foreign missionary of the Vatican; but ironically enough he genuflects simultaneously before the foreign missionary of the Kremlin.

12

SHANGHAI BLUES

Old China hands like to tell a tale of the old days when a certain British official was leaving China. Though not over-popular, courtesy demanded that the Chinese give him a farewell dinner. This was done, and chivalry required that the departing guest be speeded on his way with a kindly speech.

"Why is it," asked his Chinese host proposing the distinguished guest's toast, "that the British get on so well wherever they go? It is because they have a saying they always live up to: 'When in Rome do exactly as you do at home'!"

The old China hands, though greatly reduced in number, still contrive to live their own lives. I saw a fair number of them in Shanghai. With one of them I visited a night club, one of the few still extant in Communist China. It was filled with thoughtful Chinese businessmen and their sad-eyed women. There were more lounge suits and slit skirts within its four walls than could be found in any comparable space outside. A Filipino band wearing dinner coats and black ties played Chinese dance tunes. A decorative girl crooner sang over the microphone. Her repertoire was Chinese. And occasionally the band leader made announcements in English.

There was a sprinkling of Europeans. Once the band leader stopped to announce the departure of a British guest for Hongkong on the following day.

"Let's bid him Godspeed," he announced. And the band played "Auld Lang Syne"!

It was Ruritanian and unreal. I looked around the crowded ballroom thronged with the last sad relics of China's national bourgeoisie. Some of them were dancing. Others sat around their tables drinking and talking with what seemed an air of artificial gaiety. They smiled, but their eyes were sombre. Perhaps for a few hours that evening they dwelt in Arcadia.

When next morning I told a Communist acquaintance who was also an official where I had been, he frowned disapprovingly.

"They are the decadent bourgeoisie," he warned.

"Well, I added to their number," I countered. He was not amused.

In the vast swarming untidy metropolis of Shanghai, housing some six million people, linger more bourgeois traces than anywhere else in China. The women are noticeably better dressed. Cosmetics and lipstick are still occasionally in evidence, and the regimented *kanpu* uniform has not completely driven the Western lounge suit from the streets. We met very few Chinese outside the charmed circle in which our official occasions took us. But shopping one afternoon in a crowded store I was greeted cautiously by a Chinese who sidled up to me.

"You a member of the Indian cultural delegation?" he asked. "Yes."

"Where do you come from?"

"Bombay."

"Say," he said with sudden enthusiasm, "is business good there?"

My interpreter, who had momentarily lost me in the crowd, joined me at this juncture, and my new companion, taking one swift look at his uniform, vanished into the throng.

"For the past five months," remarked a British businessman,

"'I have had no association with any Chinese businessman.'" It was June, 1952, when the San Fan and Wu Fan movements were drawing to a close.

"That," he added, "saves both sides from embarrassment."

He himself, however, was not free from embarrassment, for when I visited him in his office I found the corridors and the anteroom plastered with placards and posters. Most of these portrayed John Bull being kicked out of China.

"They've even got me on their placards," said the businessman wryly, opening his door and pointing to a caricature of himself nailed on the office door.

He was jaunty and spruce, and his pin-striped suit was immaculate. A gardenia adorned his buttonhole. I found myself thinking of the curiously resilient character of the British, who were adapting themselves admirably to the new order of things in India and were doing the same in a vastly different context in China. To have your employees lampoon you openly in your own office was by any standards a novel experience. But the old China hand appeared to be taking it in his stride.

"I've been in this country thirty years," he remarked. "Very happy, very profitable years. I reckoned we could do business with the Communists when they came. After all, the first two things they did were to control currency and to open up communications. That meant trade—or so I thought. Now I'm not so sure."

He was frank and fair-minded. The Communists, he said, had undoubtedly done some good. Pilfering was largely a thing of the past, and there was very little corruption. "But life is very hard for the Chinese middle classes. They're caught between the devil and the deep blue sea. It's Hobson's choice for them, a choice between two evils—the corruption of the Kuomintang and the tyranny of the Communists. They've had it coming and going."

In Shanghai we had further opportunities to investigate the San Fan and Wu Fan movements. Many of their more sombre workings were high-lighted in this commercial metropolis. As in

Canton there were whisperings of daily suicides. It was clear from what we heard and from the pronouncements of many high-ranking Communist leaders that these movements signified much more than a drive against corruption. The Red hierarchy was equally worried about the corroding influence of the capitalists on the party rank and file, and the spread and infiltration of rightist thought in the leadership cadres. It seemed as if the "3-anti" and "5-anti" campaigns were primarily concerned with stopping a threatened rot in the class struggle and only secondarily concerned with corruption and other vices. Here again the voice of Kao Kang, party, government, and military boss of Manchuria, appeared to be the voice of the regime. "It is necessary," he warned, "for us to recognise the serious menace brought about by the bourgeois ideology and rightist thought, and resolutely to overcome them. Otherwise we not only shall find it impossible to implement thoroughly the government's policy for large-scale economic construction following the anti-U.S., Aid Korea campaign and the production-increase and economy drive, but also shall fail to consolidate what success we have already achieved."

These words reverberated throughout China. In Shanghai the bourgeoisie were definitely on the defensive.

In May, 1952, the British Chargé d'Affaires in Peking delivered a note to the Chinese government disclosing the decision of the British firms trading in China to close down and withdraw their staffs. The note requested facilities to do so. It also inquired whether the Chinese government would be prepared to enable British trade with China to continue even if trading inside China were rendered impossible. In other words, London appeared willing to trade with China but not in China. The note suggested the continuation of trading through an association of manufacturers and oversea buyers experienced in the China trade.

I asked a British business acquaintance whether he thought this feasible. Was the British note induced by the recent Moscow economic conference which sought to by-pass intermediaries and businessmen?

"No," he replied, "the timing was purely coincidental. Our decision was in no way influenced by that conference."

He went on to explain the developments which had led the once optimistic old China hands to revise their opinion. For some time after the Communists had entered Shanghai in May, 1949, business relations between the government and the British firms had been good.

"We knew," he said, "that two things would considerably alter the pattern of our trade with China: first, the change in her international relationship, which inclined her more to Russia and Eastern Europe; secondly, her internal economy. Naturally there would be progressively less room for private enterprise as the State economy extended its sphere. But we were hopeful we could trade for some time in and with China. She recognised her own capitalists as one of the friendly classes. And maybe, we thought, she would put up with us."

In fact British business houses in China were at first more irked by the Nationalist blockade and the bombing of Shanghai than by any hostility from the Communists. The government appeared to be willing to trade with them, and on the whole it had treated them fairly until the outbreak of the Korean War in June, 1950. From then on the Communists' attitude had grown progressively lukewarm and then hostile.

"Korea holds the key to more things in China than most people suspect," said a foreign diplomat. His view was confirmed by other knowledgeable quarters. Most of them felt that peace in Korea would ease internal and external tensions.

On the other hand, xenophobia is no new phenomenon in China. To the old distrust of the foreigner the Communists add a new and intense hate. Suspicion of the West takes pathological forms. A woman member of our delegation, having written a letter to a friend in England, inquired from one of the women interpreters what the air-mail postage would be. The interpreter glanced at the address on the envelope.

"Do you mean to say," she inquired, "that you have still an English friend with whom you correspond?"

"More than one," she was assured. It amazed and pained her.

Yet this interpreter, we discovered later, was a graduate of Columbia University. She spoke with a marked American accent.

"And how did you like your stay in America?" some of us asked.

"I hated every moment of it," she exploded.

All the same, she appeared the next morning in an American zipper blouse and produced her American-made fountain pen with a flourish.

I talked with a number of British businessmen and learned from them some of the ways of the Chinese government *vis-à-vis* the foreign trader. With the outbreak of the Korean War their position had grown markedly more difficult. They conceded that without the Korean imbroglio the government would sooner or later have launched an offensive against the capitalists. But the war had precipitated the offensive. It accorded with popular psychology, which was soon whipped to fever pitch by the Aid Korea, Resist America movement. It also fitted in with the new official scheme of things. In a sense the Wu Fan movement, which was directed against corrupt elements in the indigenous business community, was a logical culmination of the earlier drive against the foreign investor. This two-pronged attack was the regime's warning to "the enemies" within its fold.

The onslaught on the Chinese businessman was brutal and direct. Against the foreign trader it was more calculated and subtle. For nearly two years the role of the capitalist in China, foreign and indigenous, has been largely that of a contractor. Private enterprise is primarily a feeder for State enterprises. Although large-scale concerns are normally owned and operated by the State, they are conducted with the cooperation of businessmen. These trends were inevitable, for as government monopolies expanded private trade shrank.

It is difficult to assess precisely the British investments in China; nor is the matter of much relevance, because values have fluctuated greatly in the country over the past two decades. Before the war these investments were estimated in the neighbourhood of £350,000,000, of which £25,000,000 were in government bonds. On May 20, 1952, Anthony Eden, speaking in the House of Commons, said that an objective estimate of immovable British assets would be from £200,000,000 to £250,000,-000. In 1951 a Communist journal had placed the figure at £200,000,000. Since then the Shell Company and the British American Tobacco Company have disappeared from the list of foreign investors. The assets of the former were summarily requisitioned, and the latter in April, 1952, yielded its internal business, valued at £2,000,000, to the Chinese government after two years of negotiations. In August the Shanghai Dockyards and Mollers Engineering & Shipbuilding Company were requisitioned. More recently, in November, 1952, the Chinese government requisitioned the British-owned water, gas, and tram companies and the Mackenzie Company.

Whatever the extent of their assets, British businessmen are anxious to cut their losses and clear out. To continue in the present circumstances is to throw good money after bad. As contractors they find the volume and area of their business greatly restricted. But the government will not hear of them dispensing with redundant labour and compels them, even when their plants are virtually immobilised or idle, to pay every single workman on their rolls his full wage.

Inevitably a stage is reached when their tills are empty. Even then the unfortunate concerns cannot close down. In the case of an indigenous firm the government might offer to buy up its assets at the official price. But foreign firms must perforce continue to operate, and in order to do so they are compelled to import foreign exchange from home. One estimate placed this compulsory inflow at £6,000,000 in 1951. Since the small foreign trade which China has is probably paid for by foreign exchange balances, this represents a fair windfall.

Theoretically a foreign firm may wind up after paying its employees three months' wages and settling its other liabilities and dues. In practice, this entails paying a month's bonus per year of service to every employee plus about another month's wages to enable him to go home. This may total a lump payment of two years' wages to each employee apart from income tax and other imposts. Even then, the government may delay the issue of exit permits for the foreign staff. Conversely, some British businessmen who had temporarily left the country were finding it difficult when we were there to secure reentry visas. In terms of creature comforts life is still comparatively easy for most British businessmen; but they commonly work under acute mental tension.

The Chinese character abounds in contradictions. Men who are cruel to cart ponies can be kind, even tender to domestic pets. The monetary urge is (or was) strong in nearly every one of them; but most foreign residents testify to their high sense of family and fraternal duty. Paradoxically, again, if their pressure tactics towards the foreign entrepreneur are unconscionable, many British businessmen readily certify to the economic morality of the government in other ways.

I was given at least two such instances. In one a British businessman purchased Australian wool at 187 shillings at the instance of the government. The Communist official stalled for nearly five months when it came to signing the contract, and by the time he was ready the price of wool had dropped to 110. But the government paid without demur at the original rate of 187. It might be argued in this case that the government which forbids speculation could not logically profit from it.

The other instance concerned the purchase of cotton from Pakistan by a British importer on a contract with the Chinese government. Inadvertently the agreement did not provide that the buyer should pay the difference in enhanced export duty. Pakistan raised its duty, and the importer stood to lose £30,000; but the government paid without a murmur.

Peking's reluctance to enter into diplomatic relations with London is partly explained by the continuing existence of British investments in China. The ostensible reason given for the Chinese government's obduracy is the presence of a British consul at Taipeh. The real reason probably is deeper, and it seems to be connected with British investments in the country. Had the United Kingdom had an ambassador in Peking, the Communists could hardly have proceeded as far as they have without goading the British representative into invoking international law and lifting the issue to a global plane. As matters stand, the British business community is virtually helpless and unprotected. Not even the persevering patience of Leo Lamb, head of the negotiating mission, can wear down the procrastinating genius of Chou En-lai. Like Fabius, Peking plans to conquer by delay. Time is on its side.

The Chinese, I discovered, are unusually sensitive to their highly fluid relations with the British. I had an appointment one afternoon with Leo Lamb at the former British Embassy in Peking and asked Chang, one of our interpreters, for a car. He asked in turn where I was going.

"To the British Embassy."

No interpreter ever handles such a situation singly. Chang went into a huddle. He returned to my room a few minutes later with a bland, impassive countenance.

"I am sorry," he said politely, "but there is no British Embassy in China."

Realising that I had erred technically, I apologised. "I want to see Mr. Leo Lamb, head of the British negotiating mission."

Chang departed into another huddle and said smoothly when he reappeared: "I am sorry, but we do not know where he stays."

Everyone who is anyone in Peking knows that Mr. Lamb's

residence is the former British Embassy. Fortunately a colleague who happened to be in my room knew where it was. So we asked for the car, got it, and left. I learned later that many letters addressed to the British Embassy are returned by the postal authorities with the superscription "Unknown."

In the Communist view foreign investments spell political sub-servience. When China says she is willing to do business with the West on equal terms she means she is willing to do it on her own terms. Regulations notified in the newspapers have the force of law; and, being in Chinese, they lend themselves at times to more than one interpretation. British businessmen generally agreed that there was justice in the Communist courts as between a foreign and a local trader, but that the scales were weighted heavily in favour of the government when it was a party in a suit.

One businessman gave an amusing example of the arbitrary character of these regulations. He had ordered certain goods from abroad. The day before the package arrived the govern-ment by a newspaper notification ruled against the importing of a number of items, among them some that were in the business-man's package. It took him three months to obtain his parcel.

"I had to sign seventy-eight forms," he remarked, "six for each of the thirteen items in the parcel."

Without a doubt the Communist regime is allergic to the old China hands, whom it regards as archaic and visible links with a dead and forgotten past. The pinpricks and humiliations they occasionally have to endure are meant primarily to impress its own people.

"They keep talking of international law," remarked a Chinese acquaintance. "Of course, they forget that this body of law is weighted with Western influence. They were both the drafts-men and the interpreters. We have set new precedents on various international issues, particularly on those relating to foreign in-vestments."

When China sets up machinery for foreign trading, it will be to her own specifications. In all likelihood foreign trade with China will continue, as indeed it does, through the entrepôt channel of Hongkong. But meanwhile British trade within the country is shrinking rapidly. In 1939 the Hongkong & Shanghai Bank had ten branches in China. In 1952 it had three. The Chartered Bank of India, Australia & China, which had six branches, still has two, and the Mercantile Bank of India has only one.

"I cannot wind up my affairs," remarked a foreign banker, "since the Chinese are insisting on payment to old-time depositors at the government's valuation. It isn't ethical that a bank should be called upon to pay for the inflation policy of a country."

The manager of a shipping company remarked that he dared not bring his big ships into any of the Chinese ports, because these vessels ran strictly to schedule and he never knew how long the port authorities might detain a ship in harbour. He cited the case of a French ship which had come with a cargo of Czech goods to Tientsin. It had stayed in port for eight days. On the eve of departure it was informed that a seaworthiness certificate could not be granted. Another eight days elapsed before the matter was cleared up with Peking, and meanwhile the ship paid £600 a day in port charges.

History has a habit of repeating itself. In some respects the situation in 1952, so far as the British were concerned, was almost exactly as it had been in 1842. The Opium War, beginning in 1839, ended with the Treaty of Nanking in August, 1842. Some fifty years earlier George III had sent a mission to China to persuade the Emperor Ch'ien Lung to accept a British ambassador. Ch'ien Lung had haughtily declined. "Our dynasty's majestic virtue," he wrote, "has penetrated unto every country under Heaven, and Kings of all nations have offered their costly tribute by land and sea. As your Ambassador can see for himself, we possess all things. I set no value on objects strange or ingenious, and have no use for your country's manufactures. . . . It behoves you, O King, to respect my sentiments and to display even greater loyalty and submission in the future, so that, by perpetual submission to our Throne, you may secure peace and prosperity for your country thereafter."

By the Treaty of Nanking, Britain obtained Hongkong and the right to appoint consuls but no ambassador. A foreign-administered customs system was allowed. Exactly 110 years later, in 1952, Britain was still in Hongkong, had a few consuls in the country and was waiting to be permitted to appoint an ambassador in Peking. The wheel had turned full circle.

America's trade embargo, while stimulating the Communists' drive for economic self-sufficiency, has also enlarged China's trade with the Soviet Union and Eastern Europe. Simultaneously it has encouraged the Chinese belief that, for some time at least, they can get along by themselves. The hardening of the Communist attitude towards British trade is partly explained by this fact, for it is not true, as the Chinese like to suggest, that Britain's inability to place her goods in China is due entirely to her own attitude. Much was made of the Western blockade at the Moscow Economic Conference. Actually the British embargo is restricted to strategic goods, and there is nothing to prevent China extending her general trade with Britain if she so desires. The American embargo is in practice of a more comprehensive character.

The reorientation of China's economic pattern is reflected in her trade figures. In 1949 America was still the best trader with Communist China, and the Tientsin customs figures for June revealed her as heading the list of foreign exporters and importers. The picture has altered considerably since then. In 1950 imports from the Soviet Union constituted only 19 per cent of the total, but in 1951 they had risen to 45 per cent. Similarly imports from Eastern Europe, which were 1.3 per cent in 1950, rose to 25.33 per cent in the following year.

Foreign trade in Shanghai is in the doldrums. Gone is the compradore who once acted as the trading link between his country and the West. With the missionaries, opium, and the gunboat he is cast aside as yet another symbol of the bad old days. Whether the West will ever salvage its trade with Communist China is problematic. The omens are not propitious. There is room, albeit restricted, for some Western trade with China, as Britain realises; but the days when the West could trade freely within China are over.

Beggars and prostitutes no longer dot China's ports and cities. Some may say that is symbolic and significant. At one stroke the Communists are seeking to erase from their land these tawdry reminders of poverty and degradation. Steps to rehabilitate both beggars and prostitutes were among the earliest taken by the regime. Many have been transplanted to the countryside and set to work on the land in an effort simultaneously to wean them from their trades and provide them with employment. "Reformed" beggars have been known to parade the streets, dancing in celebration of their reform.

In all our journeyings through China I saw only three beggars —one in Canton and two in Shanghai. The Canton beggar was very old and diseased. One of the two in Shanghai was a deaf mute who gabbled and gesticulated for alms. The other was a White Russian woman who, I suspect, having once been a lady of easy virtue had lost her profession and was now driven to another profession also forbidden by the law. She was blowzy and vulgar but pathetic, symbol of a lost tribe from a lost country wandering through an alien land in a planet without a visa.

13

FIVE STARS

It is easy to read too much into a country's past and to see in its fables and epigrams the delineation of national character. The tales and Analects of Confucius, like the sayings of the Delphic oracle, lend themselves to a variety of interpretations. Some who hold that the Chinese have an instinctive horror for oppressive government like to recall the celebrated story of Confucius in the Tai mountains. While journeying over these mountains on his way from Lu to Chi, the sage encountered a woman weeping and wailing at a grave.

"Why do you weep?" asked Confucius.

"My husband's father," said the woman, "was killed here by a tiger, and my husband also; and now my son has met the same fate."

"But why do you not leave so fatal a spot?"

The woman sighed. "There is no oppressive government here," she said.

Whereupon Confucius, turning to his disciples, declared: "Remember this. Remember this, my children, oppressive government is fiercer and more feared than a tiger."

It is a good tale, and its moral is impeccable. But has the

story's impress burned itself on the minds of Confucius' country-men? History, some say, controverts this; and in proof they cite the fact that the genius of the Chinese people has flowered most richly under authoritarian rule. China reached glorious heights of achievement and cultural expression under her tyrants—the Sung autocrats, the Tang Empress Wu, the Manchu monarchs K'ang-hsi and Ch'ien Lung.

The Chinese peasantry constitute perhaps the most patient people on earth, and patience has always rated high among the country's traditional virtues though its place in the Communist litany of virtues is not known. Mao's regime has exploded many myths, including the myth that Chinese are indifferent and the older superstition that they are a people incapable of organising themselves. Whatever else they may disclose, the Chinese people today show no signs of indifference. They seem, if anything, impatient to consolidate their new-found strength, and they display an astonishing capacity for organisation.

Superficially there is much of the Prussian in the average Chinese, even to his love for the goose-step. The Chinese like the tramp of marching feet. They revel in flags and drums. The chime and crash of cymbals excite them. Like Junker tradition, the history of China is permeated with hate for the foreigner. The greatest single cohesive loyalty is race. This may seem surprising in and even unfair to a people who talk today of "Asian peace and friendship." But listening as they mouthed this phrase I had the odd, uneasy feeling that I had heard it elsewhere in a different context. Of course, I had. Not ten years earlier the Japanese had been talking of Asian Co-Prosperity when in fact they had meant Japanese prosperity. The Chinese phrase carries much the same menace.

China, like India, has overflowed its boundaries, and the peoples of both countries are found throughout Southeast Asia. The Sino-Indian problem is by no means limited to the 2,000 miles of rugged frontier which runs along the mountain chain separating the two lands. India faces China throughout Southeast Asia, where climate, by enervating the indigenous peoples, has allowed the foreigner fair scope. Aside from the Japanese, the Chinese and the Indians constitute Asia's two most industrious races. Traces of Hindu culture still linger in the temple at Borobudur in Java and the glories of Angkor Vat. From India too went the Buddhist creed. But China represents a more assertive, vigorous intrusion, and in almost every land of Southeast Asia her commercial impress is strong.

The vigour and violence of the Chinese mind have never been sufficiently appreciated abroad. In China the irredentist urge for the recovery of lost territories is fortified by the feeling that the cession to force has no validity in law or equity. These territories, it is urged, are still Chinese, and their Chinese residents are deemed to owe an overriding over-all loyalty to the land of their origin. Burma, Indo-China, Hongkong, Formosa, and Korea were once part of the Empire or owed it fealty, and even Kuomintang maps showed Tibet as part of Cathay's domain.

Characteristically the Communists pay great attention to the oversea Chinese, conscious that in them they have potential cells for infiltration and expansion. Malaya provides the classic case. Here two-thirds of the Chinese population are China-born transients. In Burma the old anti-Indian antipathy is slowly dying down to be replaced by growing suspicion of the colossus to the northeast. Three years ago, while journeying through Southeast Asia, I sensed the same simmering resentment of Chinese intrusion in Indonesia, Indo-China and Thailand. In all these countries the Chinese have accumulated considerable commercial interests. Antipathy to them is particularly acute in Thailand.

Peking maintains a Commission of Oversea Chinese Affairs, and its venerable woman chairman, Ho Hsiang-ning, who hobbles around with the aid of a stick, was a familiar figure at official receptions. Oversea representatives were present at the Chinese People's Political Consultative Conference which adopted the Common Programme. For many years China has drawn much political and economic sustenance from her nationals abroad.

Chinese migration is supposed to have begun some two thousand years ago in the days of Ch'in Shih Huang Ti, who added Indo-China to his empire. Since the Sung dynasty there has been a considerable flow abroad, the majority of emigrants coming from Kwangtung and Fukien. In Canton we visited the Martyrs' Memorial, reared in honour of seventy-two individuals who were done to death in the pre-1911 revolution. A statue of Liberty crowns the building and its base carries plaques testifying to the generous contributions from emigrant Chinese. Most of them came from the United States. Sun Yat-sen was educated in Hong-kong and Honolulu. And the founder of the fabulous Soongs though a native of Kwangtung emigrated as a boy to the United States.

I asked Kung Peng, director of the Information Department of the Ministry of Foreign Affairs, how she would define an oversea Chinese.

"A Chinese abroad," she replied, "who accepts Chinese nationality." She gave the number as approximately ten million.

Concern for the welfare of their emigrant population is not peculiar to the Communists for the Kuomintang was equally solicitous. The only difference is that under Peking's direction a fifth column is being steadily regimented and mobilised in many Asian lands. In 1943 the Kuomintang *China Handbook* gave the number of oversea Chinese as a little over eight and a half million. An Overseas Chinese Affairs Commission was a feature of the Kuomintang regime, which also paid great attention to the education of emigrant students. Before the war there were said to be more than 3,000 institutions of higher, secondary, and primary education for oversea Chinese scattered over forty-five countries on five continents. In 1941 the number of Chinese schools in Malaya was over a thousand. The Kuomintang used these institutions for propagating Chinese nationalism abroad. To some extent, still indeterminate, the Communists are attempting to exploit them similarly for their own ends.

That the oversea Chinese are regarded by Peking as the nuclei for Communism's shock brigades in Asia is certain. Alongside them the indigenous Communists are being adjured to lay the train for the final destruction of the "reactionary" section of the bourgeoisie. In *Internationalism and Nationalism*, written in November, 1948, a year after India had obtained her independence, Liu Shao-chi directs a call to Asian countries: "The Communists in other colonial and semi-colonial countries such as India, Burma, Siam, the Philippines, Indonesia, Indo-China and South Korea, must for the sake of their national interests similarly adopt a firm and irreconcilable policy against national betrayal by the reactionary section of the bourgeoisie, especially the big bourgeoisie, which has already surrendered to imperialism. If this were not done, it would be a grave mistake."

The "liberation of Asia" from "Imperialist and reactionary bourgeois" domination is implicit in Communist China's thinking. India, to Peking, is still a semicolonial country, not completely liberated either politically or economically. At Mukden, Kao Kang, Governor of Manchuria, inquired of Mrs. Pandit how far the British really controlled India's internal and external policies. His scepticism was undisguised when she assured him that no British control would be tolerated or was exercised. In Chinese eyes India plainly needs to be "liberated" along with the rest of Asia. The Japanese called their expansion "co-prosperity." The Chinese prefer to call it "liberation."

During our stay in Peking we were present at the inauguration of the China-India Friendship Association and heard many eloquent speeches on both sides. The Chinese interpreter's frequent reference to our "beautiful friendship" drew some involuntary smiles and set the keynote for the occasion. More than one speaker touched on the travels of the Chinese pilgrim, Hsüan Tsang, who came to India in the reign of the Emperor Harsha in the seventh century, and of an earlier visitor, Fa-Hsien, who was in India during the reign of Chandragupta II in the fifth century. The high light of the morning was a speech by Vice-Premier Kuo Mo-jo, who is China's leading littérateur. Kuo

Mo-jo has an attractive voice which gives even the monosyllabic Chinese tongue a rounded lilt. One sentence, though mellifluously delivered, struck an ambiguous, even ominous note. "We shall pay our ancestors' debts to India," he remarked with a wide smile.

When neither the Chinese nor the Russians trouble to conceal their ultimate intentions in Asia, it is surprising that many on this continent should still beguile themselves with dreams of a "beautiful friendship." In the ultimate analysis a country's foreign policy is determined by enlightened self-interest, and even if it may not be wise to hunt for peace with a gun or politic to thumb your nose at an opponent, realism requires that you should know the nature of those you deal with. At the nineteenth Soviet Communist Party Congress in October, 1952, Stalin, after dwelling upon the assistance which the Russian Communist party had received from Communist parties abroad, set about reciprocating the gesture. "Naturally," he observed, "our Party cannot remain indebted to the fraternal parties, and it must in its turn render support to them and also to their peoples in their struggle for emancipation. The Soviet Union needs the support of the peoples abroad and pledges the Soviet Communist Party to help foreign Communist and democratic parties fight for peace and liberation."

Malenkov was more specific. Speaking on October 3, 1952, over five years after India had achieved her independence, he referred to "the virtual crumbling to pieces of the colonial system of imperialism" and mentioned India as one of the countries "where the national movement for liberation was growing." Along with India he cited Malaya, the Philippines, and Indo-China.

Peking's savage reaction to the Korean Truce Plan sponsored by India in November, 1952, betrayed Communist China's conception of a "beautiful friendship." Just as "freedom" in the totalitarian vocabulary means freedom only to express your master's opinion, so a "beautiful friendship" conjures up a relationship where one partner dutifully echoes the opinions of the other. On

the Indian plan Chou En-lai paraphrased the language of Vishin-
sky even to the vituperative broadside directed at New Delhi.
China, like every other Communist country, wants friendship—
on her own terms.

The impact of Soviet precept and practice has been longer
and more direct on China than on India, and Chinese intellectuals
have been more susceptible to that influence than their Indian
counterparts. Communism responds to the practical, utilitarian
urge in the Chinese character. Unlike the Indian, the Chinese is
more interested in practice than in precept, in realities than in
ideas. The Indian mind delights in legal sophistries which interest
the Chinese not at all. It likes to toss ideas into the air and chase
them. I was interested to learn in Malaya that the estate managers
preferred the Indian as a rubber tapper to the Chinese. The
Indian, they said, had a deft, delicate touch, preserving the trees
longer than the Chinese, who was inclined to treat them roughly.
On the other hand, they greatly preferred the Chinese for such
energetic chores as jungle clearing. The difference in physical
aptitude underlines the difference in mental attitude.

Communism could also be fitted into the ideological framework of Confucianism, though its basic principles are poles apart
from Marxism. "The people," said Confucius, "may be made to
follow a course of action but not to know the reason why." To
surrender government to a tiny elite is an idea common to both
creeds. Until the twentieth century China was ruled by "an
aristocracy of learning." The stress on right conduct in private
and public life also is shared by the Confucianist and the Communist. Instead of reverence for the family head Communism
preaches reverence for the State and the party.

Both on the literary and on the political plane the influence of
Soviet Russia is of long standing and has been considerable. Like
the Chinese, as Mao Tse-tung often emphasises, the Russians
experienced several decades of hardships and tribulations before
they eventually found Marxism. "Many of China's conditions,"
he writes, "are identical with or similar to those of Russia before

the October Revolution. Both had the same sort of feudal oppression. Economically and culturally they were similarly backward, though China was the more so. In both countries alike, the more advanced people, disregarding all hardships, sought after revolutionary truth in order to restore national prosperity."

In his well-known treatise on *The People's Democratic Dictatorship* Mao recalls how prior to the birth of the Chinese Communist party in 1921 the country's intellectuals, such as Sun Yat-sen, Hung Hsiu-ch'üan, Yen Fu, and Kang Yu-wei, "looked to the West for truth." Mao recounts how the ancient imperial examination system was abolished and schools sprang up "like bamboo shoots after a spring rain." From the 1840's to the end of the First World War China looked to the West and, seeing in Japan the aptest Oriental pupil of the Occident, hoped to learn from the Japanese. Oddly enough, Soviet literature initially seeped into China through Japanese translations.

Russia's October Revolution created a considerable stir in China. "The salvos of the October Revolution," writes Mao, "brought us Marxism-Leninism." He emphasises how Sun Yat-sen had looked vainly to the "Western capitalist countries" for help. Liu Shao-chi is more critical. He describes Sun Yat-sen's world outlook at the time as "still of a bourgeois or petty-bourgeois character." Nevertheless, as Liu concludes, Sun stood for the doctrine of a national revolution which called for "arousing the people and uniting in a common struggle with all nations in the world who treat us as equals." He accordingly welcomed the October Revolution, sought Russian aid, and allied himself with the Chinese Communist party.

The beginnings of Soviet influence on China's political thought therefore coincide with the beginnings of the Russian Revolution. Many years later Mao was to write: "Only once in his lifetime did Sun Yat-sen receive international aid. This came from the Soviet Union." China, baulked by the West, turned hopefully to the friendly East. She turned to Moscow. From the Indian point of view the most interesting fact in the history of

China over the past century is the failure of her leaders to devise an indigenous panacea for internal ills. Gandhism was to provide India with a symbol and a shield. But China looked for salvation abroad.

The one man who might have led the country on national paths was Chiang. And Chiang failed dismally. The blame rests largely on himself, but part of it lies in the vacuum in which he operated. China was adrift. Driven from her old moorings by the rude blast of the West, she moved like a derelict ship. The West little knew the damage it did when trade followed the flag. Commerce reared the new Babylon of Shanghai, ruined the country's handicrafts, and while creating a parasitic urban class reduced the rural districts to destitution. For China the consequences were disastrous since Western influence destroyed Chinese thought and tradition without substituting any vital force or philosophy in their place. Communism was to fill the vacuum and give to the country and people a new vigour and vitality. There is irony in the thought that the Western democracies paved the way for Marx. Truly capitalism provides its own gravediggers.

Chiang, while fighting the West, sought sustenance from it. He renounced Buddhism for Methodism, and Christianity rated high in the ruling circles of the Kuomintang. His earlier achievements are dimmed by the blight of his later years. He all but succeeded in unifying the country. He built roads, railways, schools, and hospitals. In the twenties and part of the thirties he kept the currency fairly stable with the introduction of a uniform silver dollar. The Japanese incursion into Manchuria marked the turn of the tide. Caught in the dilemma of fighting the Japanese and simultaneously staving off the Communists, Chiang failed to do either effectively. The loss of the coastal ports and cities meant the loss of large revenues, for China's exchequer leaned heavily on the customs service. Corruption sapped the morale of the country. Inflation shattered its economic structure.

What Chiang failed to provide to his people was a moral fervour and force to replace their lost faith. In Hinduism India has a socioreligious system which has withstood the impact of foreign forays and incursions. Faced by danger or opposition, Hinduism has a habit of ossifying in self-defence. But with the crumbling of Confucian faith and doctrines the Chinese apparatus of intellectual self-defence collapsed. What had Chiang to offer instead? He had force but no ideas. Futilities such as the New Life Movement and the Anti-Opium Bureaus merely excited public ridicule. But Mao had ideas to proffer even if they were crystallised in One Big Idea. Communism, stepping into the void left by the impact of the West, fills it with new hopes and new ideas.

The Chinese share one quality with the British—a talent for borrowing ideas and adapting them to their needs. China touches nothing which she does not adjust. Confucius and Lao Tse were of China, Chinese. They were more concerned with men than with God, reflecting their countrymen's unconcern with heaven and deep concern with earth. Confucianism was not a religion but a way of life. It exuded sweet reasonableness and preached the doctrine of the golden mean. Therein lay its intellectual appeal to the Chinese, who are more interested in ethics than in religion and place humanism above the humanities. Lao Tse retreated into nature, but the fatalism of Taoism struck a responsive chord in the Chinese heart and mind.

It is noteworthy that, apart from Communism, Buddhism is the only important intellectual import that China has absorbed. Characteristically the Chinese have adapted it to their needs. Its metaphysical content is transmitted in a language of lofty scholarship and has attracted the attention of intellectuals. In the doctrine of transmigration the "common" people find solace and comfort. But in China the Buddhist stress on equality is greater than in India.

China was never wholly isolated from the world. Trade with Cathay finds a place in the Bible. In the second century of the Christian Era an embassy from the Roman Emperor, Marcus Aurelius, was received at the Han court. From Syria the Nestorians found their way into China in the seventh century; and in the eighth century the Arabs discovered the sea route to the Far East and landed at Canton. In this southern seaport stands one of Islam's most ancient mosques. From India about the same time came Buddhist missionaries and monks. There were brief contacts with the West in the Middle Ages. Tradition has it that several scions of the Ming dynasty embraced Christianity on the eve of their overthrow. Like Akbar in Mogul India, the Manchus in China looked kindly upon the Jesuits. Marco Polo was a guest of the Mongol Emperor Kublai Khan. In the sixteenth century the Portuguese, having discovered the Cape route to India, reached China and behaved with a truculence which deeply offended the Chinese, who expelled them. The Dutch and the British followed, and their behaviour was no less obnoxious. The Ocean Devils, as the Chinese labelled them, were a decidedly dangerous breed.

Under cover of trade European expansionist policies came into play. The Portuguese who were tactless enough to seize Malacca, a tributary of China, on their way to that country established themselves at Amoy, Foochow, and Canton. From there they were edged out by the irate Chinese and finally settled in Macao. The Dutch after unsuccessfully attempting to capture Amoy took shelter in Formosa but their preoccupation with Malaya and India soon compelled them to abandon China.

The British were more tenacious. Lord Macartney's mission in 1793 proved abortive and so did a second mission in 1816. The failure of the Napier Mission eighteen years later led to the Opium War and the Treaty of Nanking on August 29, 1842. Hongkong was ceded to the British; and gradually other concessions, including leased territories, extraterritorial rights, tariff privileges and treaty ports, were extracted. Between 1862 and 1890 China lost respectively to Britain and France the territories of Burma and Indo-China. In 1895 Japan annexed Formosa, and after the Russo-Japanese War of 1904–1905 Russia acknowledged Japanese rights in Korea. In 1910 Japan annexed Korea.

China's relations with Czarist Russia began in the second half of the seventeenth century when, taking advantage of the collapse of the Ming dynasty and the Manchu invasion, Russia tried to annex Chinese territory. This attempt was baulked in 1689. Around the middle of the nineteenth century Russia renewed her aggression. In 1867 France seized Cochin China, to which in 1883 she added Annam. Britain appropriated territory on the mainland opposite the island of Hongkong, and Russia secured the maritime province north of the Amur. By the end of the nineteenth century Russia had virtually annexed Turkestan and Mongolia and was disputing the territory of Manchuria with Japan. Later, England laid claim to the Yangtze valley, the economic heart of China. Russia seized North Manchuria, leaving South Manchuria to the Japanese, who also grabbed Inner Mongolia and the province of Fukien. France laid hands on Yunnan and Kwangtung while Germany claimed Shantung.

India was exposed to the exploitation of a single imperialist power, Britain, but China was subject to the tender mercies of rival and rapacious countries. She became the victim not of imperialism but of imperialisms rampant. She became the joint colony of international imperialism. In India the ruling power, while exploiting the country, developed some of its resources and immeasurably improved and expanded communications. This was not the case in China, where no single power enjoyed monopolistic privileges sufficient to induce progressive investment. Because of this China, prey to conflicting imperialisms, was drained even while she was devoured. As one commentator puts it, "imperialism played the dog in the manger."

Perhaps these differing backgrounds account for the differing development of India and China. On India was concentrated the imperial might of Britain, which held the gorgeous East in fee and regarded this dominion as the brightest jewel in the British crown. China was robbed even of reflected radiance. She was looked upon not as a cherished possession to be jealously nursed but as a victim to be indiscriminately violated.

Possibly this also explains China's deep-rooted antipathy to the West as contrasted with India's comparative tolerance. In Indian eyes nothing became Britain so much as the manner of her leaving. China, which saw extraterritorial rights relinquished by the West in 1942 in the stress of a war where their value was theoretical, had witnessed Soviet Russia shedding them voluntarily over twenty years earlier. No single act had more firmly fixed in the Chinese mind the line dividing proletarian Russia from the capitalist West. At one stroke Russia had redeemed her past and condemned the present.

The end of the Second World War found America in the invidious position of a power opposed to colonialism and Communism, and placed in China in a dubious role open to misinterpretation. The United States occupation of Japan high-lighted this dilemma. Through no fault of her own America in Japan came to be viewed as the head and fount of imperialism in the Far East. Having failed to reconcile the Kuomintang and the Communists, she was driven by the sheer logic of events, aided and abetted by her own highly amateur tactics, into appearing as the chief apologist for the discredited Kuomintang and its principal. To Mao Tse-tung and his followers the logical end to America's present campaign can only be the attempted conquest of Communist China. America is thus branded by Peking as Public Enemy Number One, and the Sino-Soviet axis proportionately gathers strength.

It must be confessed that Russia's attitude towards Communist China has generally been correct. Moscow might have chosen to hand over Manchuria to the Chinese Communists following the Soviet's nine days' war with Japan. Instead the Russians, evacuating Manchuria in stages, handed it over to the Kuomintang troops after denuding the factories of much of their installation and equipment. Admittedly they connived at the Chinese Communist troops' infiltrating simultaneously into the Manchurian countryside. The only explanation for this is that the Russians underestimated the Communists even more than did the Americans. In 1945, according to Harry Hopkins, Stalin held no great opinion of Mao Tse-tung's chances of success.

Mao's revolution, contrary to Marxist orthodoxy, was spearheaded by the peasants, not by the proletariat. In India the revolution was inspired by what the Communists would call "a bourgeois or petty-bourgeois outlook." It was led largely by the urban educated classes helped by the restive white-collar workers and supported spasmodically by the urban proletariat and the peasants. Its chief strength was derived from the middle and lower middle classes. The closest Chinese political parallel to Gandhi is Sun Yat-sen if one excludes Hung Hsiu-ch'üan, leader of the Taiping rebellion. Yet it is noteworthy that both these Chinese leaders drew inspiration from external sources rather than relying on their own internal strength. Therein they contrast sharply with Gandhi, who in nonviolent noncooperation forged an Indian weapon for Indian needs. Hung Hsiu-ch'üan was inspired by a vague mystical Christianity and called himself the "Younger Brother of Jesus Christ." Sun Yat-sen, after vainly canvassing Western aid, sought and obtained Soviet help and cooperation.

It might, of course, be argued that the idea of using moral suasion rather than force is not new, and that Gandhi in his thinking was undoubtedly influenced by Tolstoy, Thoreau, and Ruskin. But the weapon he forged and used on a mass scale was unique and peculiarly suited to Indian character and conditions. Never before had nonviolence been employed by a people as a weapon in its fight for political freedom. Despite years of subjugation India had in Hinduism a system robust and resilient enough to draw strength from its own fountainhead. In China the collapse of Confucianism created a vacuum in whose void the Chinese intellectual roamed, as one observer puts it, "like a displaced person emotionally and intellectually." Chinese thought, exposed to many conflicting blasts, suddenly found itself rootless.

It is Mao's distinct contribution to the Communist cause that in transplanting it he was careful to graft it on a Chinese stalk and give it a Chinese look. But even Mao has made no secret of his basic loyalty to Russia. The irony of the Western intrusion in China is that in attempting separately and jointly to cancel out China the Western powers cancelled out themselves. "Imperialist invasions," Mao has written, "shattered Chinese illusions about learning from the West. Was it not strange that the teachers should always be encroaching upon their pupils?"

Thus the conversion of the old anti-West feeling into a strong pro-Soviet loyalty represented a smooth and logical process. The eclectic streak in the Chinese character saw nothing irrational in the transition. And the process in any case dated from the very foundation of Soviet rule with the October Revolution. The accident of Chiang's association with the West, particularly America, fixed these conflicting loyalties in fierce focus and gave them heat and fury.

Mao has described Marxism-Leninism as "a universal truth which is applicable anywhere." He seeks to give it a Chinese visage. "Follow the path of the Russians—this was the conclusion," he writes. To him neutrality is merely a camouflage, and a third road does not exist. In plumping definitely for one side against the other he is doing something which the practical Chinese mind, impatient of metaphysical niceties, understands and appreciates. But in India the very force which prompted her people to rely on themselves in their battle for freedom now leads them to lean again on themselves and eschew the contending blocs. Perhaps this is what Nehru means when he insists that his policies spring from Indian traditions and are rooted in Gandhian teaching.

14

GANDHI, NEHRU, AND MAO

I shall always remember my last interview with Gandhi. It was at Panchgani, a hill station not far from Bombay. And it took place at night.

The flickering light of a kerosene lamp cast strange patterns on the wall. Gandhi sat, as he always did, on the floor in a white loincloth and shawl. His disciples stirred restively in the shadows around him. There was something slightly eerie in the atmosphere —until Gandhi spoke.

That soft, sane voice. In an aside during the interview, which was concerned with political matters, he spoke of the importance of means and ends. "The means matter," he said with the intense earnestness which his voice and eyes sometimes simultaneously conveyed. "Bad means make for bad ends." I had often read his writings on that theme, but this was the first time I had heard him speak about it.

It would be reassuring to say that in my journeyings through Mao's China I recalled this episode. The truth is that I never did. But when I sorted out impressions later something stirred in subconscious memory, and like Saul I saw the light in a blinding flash. The means and the ends.

To many sophisticated, Westernised Indians, Gandhi's views on politics and economics, because they are fundamental, appear to be elementary. The basic tenet of his creed is reverence for the individual. "The truest test of democracy," he writes, "is in the ability of anyone to act as he likes, so long as he does not injure the life or property of anyone else. It means complete freedom of opinion and action without interference with another's right to equal freedom of opinion and action."

In Gandhi's reckoning, the animate personality of the individual ranks higher than the inanimate being of the State. Freedom of opinion and action is an elementary right of every citizen. From this springs a reciprocal regard for the acts and opinions of others and a respect for human life and property. Here the Mahatma stands poles apart from Marx and Mao.

Reverence for the individual shines strongest in his political teachings, for blended in the doctrine of ahimsa, or nonviolence, are two of Christianity's major principles: the precept of returning good for evil, and the promise that the meek shall inherit the earth. The idea of using moral suasion rather than force is, of course, not new to humanity; but to the Mahatma belongs the credit of attempting to employ it as an instrument for political and social regeneration.

Gandhi was always anxious to emphasise that satyagraha, or nonviolent resistance, is the weapon of the strong, not the weak. He used to explain how, by enduring the maximum suffering without thought of counterviolence, the true exponent of satyagraha seeks to shame the wrongdoer into doing right. In the process he injures no one physically but himself. He demonstrates the will to suffer in order to convert his opponent. Hatred has no place in his scheme of things. As a result, the opponent is not physically coerced. He is morally undermined. Inevitably, class hatred or class war is anathema to this creed. Far from thinking of the uplift of the masses in terms of conflict of the classes, Gandhism sets out to compose their differences peacefully.

Gandhi was a theist. As a staunch Hindu he believed in the spiritual nature of man; but his concept of religion as a moral force transcended creed. In Nehru's words, he gave to Hinduism "a kind of universal attire." He liked to interpret the life of Christ as a triumphant vindication of the principle of nonviolence. India's ancient rishis, or wise men, regarded religion as self-realisation. Gandhi also saw it as the striving of the human personality to express itself in service, suffering, and sacrifice. "You cannot divide social, political, and purely religious work into watertight compartments. I do not know any religion apart from human activity."

Marxism, some say, also represents a religion of human activity and service. But with two vital differences: it denies freedom to the individual, which is the core of Gandhism; and it rejects theism, which the Mahatma cherished. Moreover, it permits violence to one's opponents, and this cuts at the roots of Gandhian teaching.

In certain respects Mao resembles Gandhi—but only superficially. To the Indian leader as to the Chinese, the basic fact of economics is that man must eat. Like Gandhi, Mao has always seen in foreign exploitation one of the main causes of the degradation of his country's poor. And both men share the common quality of never standing apart from the people, though Mao's State would mould its citizens in the Marxist image. Like Gandhi again, Mao has profound understanding and respect for the peasantry. But neither, I am sure, would appreciate the other's idiom or approve of his methods.

If the Mahatma taught India anything, he taught her that man does not live by bread alone. He would dismiss as vulgar the notion that a regime's responsibility ends with the mere provision of bread and circuses. Marxism identifies the individual's weal with the State's whim. It denies to the individual the right to make his own mistakes, allowing him only the right to repeat the dictator's errors. To Gandhi, individuals were more important than governments; and on many occasions vital political discussions with colleagues were held up while the Mahatma gravely offered advice or solace to a stranger in distress.

The means and the ends. Gandhi laid great store by the means, though with the fatalism of the orthodox Hindu he was prone to regard the ends as being outside human control and determined only by divine guidance. Yet in so far as he saw ends as a projection of means it was logical for him to argue that bad means make for bad ends. His means were often ends. A method, non-violence, became with him a mission.

The one thing that distinguishes the Indian leader from the Chinese is the Mahatma's concern for the individual as against Mao's stress on the State. Here is crystallised the antithesis between democracy and Communism, because Gandhi, despite his idiosyncrasies, his love of personal power, his proneness to idealise the *status quo* and to indulge in the mystic and the medieval, was by instinct a true democrat: he cared passionately for the personality of the individual.

Though he preached a simple creed Gandhi was a complex, even a complicated man. The phenomenon he presented of a preeminently spiritual prophet who was also a predominantly political leader puzzled and piqued many of his own countrymen. Some—including Nehru—could not accept nonviolence as an article of faith. Yet here, again, Gandhi's distinctiveness stems from this faith which, by disavowing all forms of hatred, made it impossible for him to be a Marxist. Many of the world's great personages have entered men's minds only to destroy human fellowship and good will. It is Gandhi's great contribution to the civilisation of his day that he sought not to destroy, but to promote in men's hearts a love for their fellow men.

How much of Gandhi's heritage does Nehru really represent? The question is often asked, not only in India but abroad.

Of the many times I have seen Gandhi and Nehru together over the years one comes back vividly. It was at the meeting of the Congress in Bombay in the fateful August of 1942 when, overnight, the entire Congress executive was clapped into jail. Nehru, on the rostrum, was speaking of India's poor. "There is nothing beautiful about poverty," he said passionately. "I hate poverty."

It was an oblique though unconscious rebuke to the Mahatma's idealisation of poverty. At the centre of the platform sitting bent over a document, Gandhi looked up quickly. He smiled. In the fleeting smile was all the affectionate indulgence of a father for a slightly wilful son. The next moment he was immersed again in his papers.

Nehru had admitted that he did not give absolute allegiance to nonviolence or accept it forever; but, he stated at another time, "it attracted me more and more, and the belief grew upon me that, situated as we were in India and with our background and traditions, it was the right policy for us." He added: "A worthy end should have worthy means leading up to it."

Jawaharlal has the habit of rationalising what his mind does not initially and easily accept. So he says of nonviolence: "That seemed not only a good ethical doctrine but sound, practical politics, for the means that are not good often defeat the end in view and raise new problems and difficulties." Here is the pragmatic approach to nonviolence as opposed to Gandhi's absolute and immutable faith; but, significantly, Nehru accepts without qualification the Gandhian interpretation of means and ends. To him also the means matter.

The rebel in Gandhi and his ability to inject backbone and character into the Indian masses first drew Nehru to the Mahatma's side. Nehru, reluctant to accept many of the older man's premises, was impressed by the results until in time he was content to surrender his will on most major issues to the Mahatma. The conflict between heart and head which has grown to be part and parcel of Nehru's being dates from this period. It survives the Mahatma's death.

In his autobiography Nehru quotes a revealing passage from Henry James: "If your heart does not want to, your head will assuredly not make you believe." And he goes on to write: "The emotions govern the general outlook and control the mind. Our conversations, whether they are religious, political or economic, are really based on emotion or instinct." Here again is an attempt to rationalise his emotions. Always there is this conflict between heart and head. Like Hamlet, Nehru is noble and vacillating.

So long as Gandhi lived, the intellectual struggle within the younger man was subordinated to what he believed were the larger interests of the country and the Congress. He could not share the Mahatma's views on machinery and modern civilisation. He found it difficult to accept Gandhi's theory that private wealth constituted a trust; and, though he accepted nonviolence as a weapon in the battle for freedom, he was reluctant to accept it as a creed. A Brahmin by birth, he was impatient with Gandhi's idealisation of caste. He had renounced wealth for patriotism, but he believed neither in renunciation nor in asceticism. A former colleague comments: "No Hound of Heaven dogs his step."

Nehru none the less saw in the Mahatma a luminosity of patriotism and purpose which compelled his loyalty. His loyalty survived the stresses and strains of minor differences and divergences. Within Gandhism's moral framework Nehru sought to contain his material impulses.

The contradictions were unresolved, and with Gandhi's passing the conflict projected itself on another plane. From the purely personal and national field it moved to the international sphere. Nehru has never been at home with himself. In him the intellect has always conspired with the emotions and plunged his being into a vortex of internal tumult. Long ago he confessed that he felt ill at ease in the intellectual climate of his country. His habit of mind is essentially Western. During his last term of imprisonment in 1942 Nehru shared a cell with the well-known Muslim Congressman, Maulana Azad, who is now Education Minister in the Government of India. Azad relates how Nehru talked in English during his sleep. "He not only thinks and talks in English," wrote Azad. "He dreams in English."

Nehru is a patrician whose heart is with the plebs. Though an intellectual by training his temperament makes him an easy prey to emotion. Like Gandhi he is an individualist; and he shares the Mahatma's reverence for the human personality. But the Welfare State looms large in his economic calculations, and he loves to browse over blueprints and plans. Despite his proud, assertive nationalism he has done more than any other single leader to make India international-minded. He saw in Gandhi not only a contrast but a challenge. His being responded. The rational part of his nature sublimated the revivalist in the Mahatma.

Gandhi's economic and political thinking betrayed great gaps. Much of it was influenced by his immediate environment, and the permutations and combinations of international politics and economics interested him very little. His own thinking operated on a different plane. In many small ways he was also curiously uninformed. "Who is Charlie Chaplin?" he is reported to have inquired when asked to meet the famous film star in London.

Nehru's mind looks out through wide windows on wide horizons. Unlike Gandhi—who used to call his own intuition his "inner voice"—his touchstone has been study and thought more than experience. Experience has coloured his outlook, intensified his emotions, and influenced his mental and moral fibre. The strange thing is that Nehru, a man primarily of impulse and emotion, has done more than most people in India to foster the habit of thought.

Is he a Marxist? I think the Marxist colouring in Nehru's thought derives principally from the fact that as a young man he became convinced of the Marxist dictum that imperialism is the product of capitalism. The feeling grew upon him and has remained that an antiimperialist must therefore be both a nationalist and a socialist. Today he is a socialist only in so far as he believes in a mixed economy which, while allowing private enterprise a place in the national scheme of things, would enlarge the frontiers of State planning. He is a nationalist only in the sense of being a patriot. If Gandhi made Indians aware of themselves, Nehru has made Indians aware of others. Gandhi woke up India to the degradation of slavery and showed her how she could hold her head erect again. Even while India struggled for her own freedom Nehru made his countrymen aware of other countries, such as Abyssinia, China, Spain, and Czechoslovakia, which in the immediate prewar years fought in the darkness of an oppression different from theirs. Nehru's record as a democrat would stand comparison with that of any of his famous contemporaries. He declined to meet Mussolini at a time when Mr. Churchill saw many glittering qualities in the Duce; and in his reckoning Czechoslovakia was not a remote, far-off place—as Mr. Neville Chamberlain suddenly discovered on the eve of Munich.

Communism in practice repels him, particularly its violence; but undeniably the idea of Marx as one who surveyed history as a scientist has an intellectual flavour which attracts him. On the other hand he has no illusions about the dictatorial nature of Communism. In a letter to his daughter Indira he distinguishes between three types of dictatorships—the Communist, the Fascist, and the military: "All these dictatorships and their variations," he notes, "are the direct opposite of democracy and the parliamentary form of government."

The tragedy of Nehru is this eternal conflict between heart and head. The phrase "I don't know" runs like the refrain of a Greek chorus through his speeches and writings. In Gandhi's day he tried to reconcile the more conservative precepts of his master with his own radical urges—to reconcile, as an erstwhile Congress colleague put it, the holy and the heroic, the claim of the moral and the call of the material. Intellectually he has never resolved the dilemma; and the paradox persists though in an altered form. Nehru's concern for the economic underdog inclines him to a sympathy for the Soviet and Chinese experiments even while he sees their totalitarian cast. His passion for the political underdog remains; but, transcending the narrow nationalist plane, it now expresses itself in an Asian assertiveness stemming from the memory of once having shared the agony of colonial domination. Today he is caught in the paradox of reconciling Gandhism with Socialism, of equating the West's concept of individual freedom with the East's concern for social and economic justice. The days when he was "prewar Harrow and postwar Moscow" are far away, but their aura lingers. Nehru sees India not as the battleground but as the bridgehead between East and West.

The contrast between Gandhi and Nehru on the one hand and Mao on the other makes an engaging analytical study. If Mao knows anything, he knows his mind. In an odd way he combines some of the qualities of both Gandhi and Nehru. He has Gandhi's earthiness, a flavour of the soil and an understanding of the peasantry which derives from experience but is also instinctive. He exudes a bland benignity much as Gandhi radiated gentleness; and his amber eyes, searching and shrewd, can—like those of the Indian leader—suddenly be stony. Gandhi's ruthlessness stemmed from a refusal to compromise with first principles. Mao's is the ruthlessness of a strategist who sees the objective clear but suits his tactics to the occasion. To him the ends are paramount. "Dogmas," he once declared, "are more useless than cow-dung. Dung can at least be used as a fertiliser."

In Panikkar's drawing room shortly after our arrival in Peking, I passed the better part of a morning with him discussing Marxist dialectics and Mao. As always Panikkar bristled with analogy and precedent. "How would I describe Mao? He is Nehru plus ruthless peasant." It was a glib analogy, but with some truth.

Mao is credited by many with less subtlety than he possesses, and the mistake which Chiang Kai-shek made of regarding him as a rustic lingers surprisingly in some quarters. The Chinese leader is no yokel even if he has the personal habits of a peasant. They say he spits and hawks and likes to munch sunflower seeds. Mao's nonchalant custom (which Edgar Snow relates) of taking off his trousers in company merely in order to make himself comfortable on a hot day has by now acquired the proportions of a legend.

With these habits, real or apocryphal, go an extraordinary sense of personal dignity and an aura of power. His presence fills a room. In Peking we were entertained at a banquet by Chou En-lai in the same building where later we met Mao. The contrast between the mandarin and the peasant was striking. It reminded me of the old saw about a Cambridge and an Oxford man. "An Oxford man walks down the street as if it belongs to him, a Cambridge man as if he didn't care to whom it belonged." Chou walked through the room as if it belonged to him. Mao's air was of one who didn't care to whom the room belonged. His bearing is faintly imperious and the measured, lumbering stalk in his stride gives him the mien of an emperor.

Environment colours character and outlook, and its influence on Mao and Nehru evokes some uneasy parallels and contrasts. Both men have read and thought deeply. Nehru's intellectual outlook derives largely from the West, from men as vastly different as Mill and Marx; but his personal philosophy, particularly in the realm of individual and social ethics, is influenced greatly by the humanism of Gandhi. Paradoxically enough, Mao's roots are nearer his own soil. He talks and thinks like a Chinese.

For the most part Nehru's Eastern sprigs are grafted on a Western stem. Aside from Gandhi, it is difficult to think of any Indian who has influenced his mind greatly. But Mao, also influenced by Western writers, notably Marx and Spencer, sees them through Chinese eyes. He sees them through the Analects of Confucius and the ballads of China's wandering minstrels, through the poetry of Ai Ching and the peasant airs of Ke Chung-ping, through Han Yu and the novels of Lu Hsun.

Confucius is China's Delphic oracle, and many of Mao's utterances echo evocatively the sayings of the sage. Near Kü-fow is his tomb, and there I heard the great man described by a Communist guide as "the Sage of feudal China but worthy of our esteem." So he should be. If Confucius thought of Society as an ordinance of Heaven where the ruler was entitled to his subjects' submission, he also stressed the need for benevolence and right-eousness in those who exercise authority. He seldom spoke of spiritual beings. "When you cannot serve men," he once re-marked to the inquisitive Tze-lu, "how can you serve spirits?"

Time and again Mao uses the Confucian idiom to convey his Marxist thought. He makes his point in harsh, homely similes, distilling the sage's maxims and sentient sayings in purposeful political prose. Mao is also a poet, and while his imagery betrays a vivid, virile imagination it has nothing of idealism. He has always been realistic and resolute. "A revolution is no invitation to a banquet," he once remarked. Behind the bland benignity is a mind, subtle and resourceful, able to translate principles into policies and to give even a foreign ideology a Chinese habitation and a name.

With Nehru, Marxism is an academic exercise. Mao sees it as a practical panacea for many ills and as a system adaptable to his country's needs without losing its basic flavour and form. The differing backgrounds of the two partly account for this differ-ence in attitude. The Chinese leader, although the son of a fairly well-to-do peasant, has walked with hardship and danger through the greater part of his life. Nehru, reared in a patrician house-hold, has also known suffering and has spent many years in prison; but he still discusses Marxism in the manner of one who regards it as an idea rather than a reality. Here is an interesting contrast between the Indian's metaphysical habit of mind and the severely practical outlook of the Chinese. Nehru treats Marxism as a fit subject for fundamental research. Mao is more interested in its possibilities of application. When during the war Nehru said that black-marketeers should be hanged to the nearest lamp post he was using a figure of speech. When Mao says it he means it.

Nehru is emotionally eruptive and has his explosive outbursts, but violence has no place in his personal or political thinking. Mao, capable of lethal language, is also capable of lethal action.

If it is necessary that heads should roll in the dust, roll they must. "No, comrade, Communism is not love," he said, chiding a too idealistic visitor. "Communism is a hammer which we use to destroy the enemy."

Mao's habit of preaching Communism in a Chinese idiom has misled many into thinking that his Marxism is different and distinct from the Moscow brand. Both sides have tended to oversimplify the picture. At one time Chinese Communism was idealised as agrarian reform; and, though the landlord falls today in the category of the three Unfriendly Classes, the notion persists that Marxism as practised in China is a growth peculiar to the country. Others contend that Communism was not only exported by Moscow into China but imposed by the Kremlin on the country.

Neither view is valid though each contains a substratum of fact. Undoubtedly Moscow is the fount of Peking's inspiration; but in terms of material aid Mao has received far less from the Russians than Chiang from the Americans. Cynically enough, Molotov signed a treaty with Chiang's brother-in-law, Dr. T. V. Soong, as late as August, 1945; and Stalin in his role of political Pilate disdained Mao's men at Potsdam and turned to the Kuomintang.

When the Communists ushered in their Common Programme in the autumn of 1949 many outsiders saw in China's composite Central People's Government, in her retention of private capital and the system of peasant proprietorship a new variant of the Marxist gospel according to Mao. Actually it was the old version, preached by Mao as far back as January, 1940, in *The New Democracy*. In it the Chinese leader clearly visualised an interim between the disappearance of the feudal China of Chiang's days and the nirvana of a Socialist China on the Soviet model. In other words the present phase, both politically and economically, represents the penultimate stage on the road to Moscow. There is nothing Fabian in Mao's theory of the inevitability of gradualness. On the political plane the Central People's Government, with its non-Communist elements, cannot be called a coalition government as the democracies use the term. Acceptance of the Common Programme implies acceptance of basic Communist policy.

In a statement published on July 1, 1949, Mao describes the people's democratic dictatorship as the combination of "democracy among the people" and "dictatorship over the reactionaries." He had early deprecated the habit of "trying to do everything at once." Increased production is China's prime need. For the present, therefore, the rich peasant must be tolerated in the countryside, and the capitalist in the city. But this phase (which conceivably may last a long period) will pass when finally the land is collectivised and the capitalist is merged and disappears in a full-fledged Socialist State spearheaded by the proletariat.

Ruthlessness, realism, and resolution. Mao's character and career are governed by these three R's. He has realised the error in a country like China, where nearly 85 per cent of the people are landless or feudal tenants, of transplanting wholesale the theory and practice of Marxism as it operates in the industrial West. In his book *Remaking of Ideology* he writes: "We study Marxism-Leninism not because of its good looks nor because there is any magic in it, as if it were a kind of charm to cast out devils. It has neither good looks nor magic; it is only very useful." And in his treatise *On Coalition Government*, published five years later, he skilfully deploys his gift for homely similes. "A room," he writes, "should be dusted, or it will be covered with dust. One's face should be regularly washed, or it will be dirty. This is also true of the ideology of our comrades and the work of the Party, which should also be constantly cleaned."

China, he feels, should never be static. Nor should Communism. Mao's own war of liberation was heterodox in the sense that it was largely an agrarian revolt which the proletariat only assisted in its final phases. It thus ran counter to the dogma of the *Communist Manifesto*. But Lenin had early preached the doctrine of adaptability; and, though the Kremlin frowned on some phases of the Chinese Revolution, Mao, with Talleyrand, discovered that nothing succeeds like success. Today the Men of Moscow scan Peking's strategy and see in it a blueprint which with some adjustments might be adapted for the "liberation" of Asia.

Mao's own views on his relations with Moscow are rooted in the political, economic, and social ethos of China which led up to the present situation. While basically loyal to the Communist thesis he likes to stress China's national independence and integrity and his own Asian background. Panikkar tells of an interview with Mao shortly after the Chinese leader's return from Moscow in 1950. Mao recalled seeing a huge airplane plant in Russia which kept turning out planes by the minute.

"Not until your country and mine can do this," he remarked, "can we act decisively. Until then we must move slowly."

The Chinese leader was not thinking merely in terms of India and China. Obviously he was thinking in terms of backward Asia. That he regards China as the leader of Asia is increasingly obvious; and sooner or later his Asian sensitivity, which now expresses itself in antiimperialism and antifeudalism, must project itself into a move for the economic "liberation" of Asia's independent countries from the "tyranny" of capitalism. Viewing imperialism through Marxist eyes, he sees it as the evil spawn of capitalism. Capitalism, he feels, is on the way out, but here and there its excrescence survives. "To sit on the fence," he said in July, 1949, "is impossible; a third road does not exist. . . . Not only in China but also in the world without exception, one either leans to the side of imperialism or socialism."

There is no doubt on which side Mao leans. Unlike Nehru, he sees situations clearly in terms of black and white, with no nuance or half-shade. A thing is wholly good or wholly evil. The ends matter. Means count for little. "Internationally," he declared in the same statement of July, 1949, "we belong to the antiimperialist front headed by the U.S.S.R. and we can look only for genuine friendly aid from that front."

Yet clearly he does not equate China with Russia's East European partners, and he sees himself in the role of an ally, not a satellite. The orthodox Russian Communist humbly reads *The Selected Works of J. V. Stalin.* In China *The Selected Works of Mao* constitute the Bible of every good Communist. Mao's dialectic approach to problems is sufficiently individualistic to make him complementary, not subordinate, to the oracle of the Kremlin as a theoretician; but the overriding loyalty of the Hunanese to the Georgian remains, and China under Mao will operate strictly within the ambit of Moscow. If anything, China, now on the ideological periphery of the Communist circle, will draw closer to the centre.

Peking has been at pains to disabuse the Chinese people of the wide impression that the Sino-Soviet Treaty of August, 1945, which was signed by the Kremlin with the Kuomintang is an "unequal treaty." And the Soviet denudation of industrial plants in Manchuria has been carefully played down. In October, 1949, the U.S.S.R. broke off diplomatic relations with the government of Chiang Kai-shek, and in February, 1950, a thirty-year Treaty of Friendship and Alliance was signed between Peking and Moscow. The Stalin-Mao axis came into being. Since then Peking has drawn noticeably closer to the Kremlin, and Chou En-lai's visit to Moscow in the autumn of 1952 saw a further strengthening of bonds.

Mao, toeing the current Marxist line and in a sense disavowing his own past, is increasingly eager to acknowledge the urban proletariat as the kingpin of his revolution. Forgetful of the fact that not until he was safely ensconced in the seat of the Manchus did Moscow's mandarins pay court to him, Mao thanks them effusively for favours rendered. These were conspicuously small but will probably increase as the Moscow-Peking axis gains in stability and strength.

Nehru, watching events from his perch in New Delhi, is conscious of their complicated pattern. That does not ease his problems. The debauch of India's pre-independence era has induced the headaches of freedom. Nehru has proclaimed his policy of seeing Asia rid of the last vestige of European domination, and this accords with Mao's view. Nehru, like Mao, sees in imperialism the degrading symbol of Asia's subservience. Its debris still litters some corners of the Orient, and like deadwood it must either be reduced to nothing or go. Here, Asian sentiment is overwhelmingly behind both men. And here, paradoxically enough, the West, like Nehru, is caught in the cleft of a dilemma.

To do or not to do, says Nehru. To go or not to go, says the West. Freedom, as Nehru rightly urges, is the strongest bastion against Communism. Had India, Pakistan, Burma, Ceylon, and Indonesia not been politically independent, Nehru and Soekarno, like Ho Chi Minh, might today have been the leaders of a liberation movement directed from Moscow and Peking. Millions of their countrymen, the vast majority, would have supported them. Significantly, the only three hot spots of Communist virulence in Asia are politically dependent countries—Indo-China, Malaya, and Korea. The last, caught in the vise of United Nations conflicts and contradictions, is paying a gory price.

Force solves nothing and masters nothing, as Nehru learned long ago from the Mahatma. Force is certainly not the answer to Communism. In Asian thinking Communism can be overcome only by countering the conditions which create it. War is a luxury the Orient cannot afford, for another war must dislocate and depress its precarious level of living and thereby aggravate the very conditions in which Communism thrives. The West sees security in terms of guns and money, which together spell power. And power means peace. Stalin also believes in the big battalions, and here he has the advantage. He can arm Russia to the teeth, and no one outside the Politburo need be the wiser. He can press a button in the Kremlin and set the Soviet Moloch on the march. Democracy rearms with flags flying and drums beating, and before the American President can secure a sizable appropriation he must go through the ballyhoo of the press on the one hand and the complicated motions of debate in the Congress on the other.

Asia sees the matter differently. To her, economic betterment means strength, which means security, which means peace. The Europe of prewar days could choose between guns and butter. For postwar Asia the choice is between guns and bread.

This is the rationale of Nehru's thinking. Inclined by temperament and training to the West, he is irked and irritated by its imperialist urges in countries such as Indo-China. He does not appreciate sufficiently the new imperialism of Soviet Russia. War seems to him to be a lunatic solution to the world's ills. Have men, he reflects, learned nothing from the shambles of two global conflicts? War may make the rich richer and the strong stronger —though even this is doubtful. But it can only make the poor poorer and the weak weaker. Asia stands to lose much if not all. Hence her vast clamant consuming hunger for peace, which the Indian leader expresses and symbolises.

Nehru is not deceived by mere protestations of peace. Familiar with Communist technique in India, he can detect the wolf for all the sheep's clothing. What concerns and disturbs him is that the West masquerading in wolf's clothing should so conduct itself in the East as often to be mistaken for the wolf.

Nehru's is the dilemma of many good men. Like him, the West protests its good intentions. But neither goodness nor good intentions are enough.

15

INDIA AND CHINA

Legalism is foreign to the Chinese mind. This is not surprising. Years of foreign rapacity have taught the Chinese that the law is very often as circumstances compel it. What, they ask, was the sanction behind the grant of extraterritorial rights and treaty port concessions except the sanction of force? The law, like God, is too often on the side of the big battalions.

In Peking's reckoning General MacArthur's advance on the Yalu River, and not the Chinese reaction to it, was an act of aggression. Korea has long been a dagger pointed at the flank of China. From this springboard the Japanese had jumped into Manchuria. China's ties with this country go back to the Han period, and during the Tang epoch Korea was a Chinese domain for two hundred years. The Mings wrestled with the Japanese for its possession. Korea has never been an independent entity in the Far East, having owed suzerainty at one time or another to China or Japan. The American government, already committed to the support of the rival government of Chiang Kai-shek, could not possibly have expected the Communists to acquiesce in the building of bases and the mounting of an offensive on their doorstep. Was it aggression to cross the threshold in order to protect the door?

So the Chinese argue. And in the minds of Asian countries stirred by memories of imperialist aggression in the past the argument rings a bell. If the North Korean invasion of South Korea in June, 1950, took the Americans by surprise there is some reason to believe that the Chinese were equally taken aback. For quite twenty-four hours Peking's propaganda machine was silent, which seems to indicate that even if the North Korean plan were known to the higher ranks in the Chinese government the knowledge had not seeped down to the lower echelons who were unprepared.

Whatever be the facts of the case, there is no denying that China is war-weary. Observers inside the country remarked how public fury and fervour had been whipped up by the Aid Korea, Resist America campaign so that when General MacArthur advanced on the Yalu the campaign mounted naturally to a crescendo of war. On the other hand, the Koreans have for many years been identified in the minds of Chinese villagers as dope peddlers and Japanese stooges. It is said that Peking found some difficulty in explaining to its new recruits from the rural areas how the Koreans had suddenly blossomed into friends and allies of the Chinese.

China would like an easing of the tension in Korea in so far as it would not involve a continual and heavy drain on her man power and resources. In other words, she wants neither war nor peace but a state of stalemate calculated to tie up the United Nations forces in Korea without placing too much stress and strain on her own economy. Does the West think likewise? Does it feel that any easing of the pressure in Korea would release Chinese troops for involvements elsewhere, notably in Indo-China?

So far, Chinese expansionism has sought economic forms, the country's nationals abroad being content to earn their livelihood in commerce and trade. This applies equally to Indian emigrants. The establishment of the Communist regime in China threatens to alter the complexion of oversea Chinese activities. And there is reason to believe that the change is even now under way. China has too many internal problems to permit any great indulgence in external military adventures. So long as she is able to operate through her fifth columns overseas, it is unlikely that she will expend her energy otherwise. The proceedings of the nineteenth Soviet Communist Party Congress in Moscow in October, 1952, when Stalin promised reciprocal support to Communist parties abroad are interesting and suggestive. They portend the shape of things to come.

In India, as elsewhere, internal Communist activities are likely to intensify if Moscow means what it says. It usually does. That India's Communists look to Peking for encouragement by proximity while eyeing Moscow worshipfully from a distance is evident from their continued tom-tomming of Mao's regime, a practice in which many genuine Indian nationalists have allowed themselves to be inveigled. The habit of denigrating the indigenous government's achievements has grown greatly in India. And by comparisons, often subtly stressed, China benefits. What many honest people do not realise is that such unflattering comparisons carry wider implications than may be immediately obvious.

In Asia the systems of democracy and Communism are on trial. China is committed to Communism. In India the impact of Western liberal ideas fell on more fruitful soil; and India with traditions of democratic rule behind her, rooted in her ancient panchayats, or village councils, took kindly and easily to democratic ways. Freedom of expression, the rule of law and representative government accord with her pattern of life and thought, and the Constitution of free India draws heavily from the practice of countries such as the United States, Canada, Britain, and Switzerland. Independent India's first general elections in 1951–1952 saw more than 160,000,000 people go peacefully to the polls, and the fact that the atmosphere was free from major incidents or strife was a remarkable tribute to the democratic spirit of the people. When it is added that the elections were held under adult franchise with a population less than 20 per cent literate the magnitude of the achievement is realised.

By a queer quirk of fate Asia's two most densely populated countries, which are also neighbours, are the testing grounds for two differing and contending political philosophies. If China proves that her system of government ensures economic security to the vast mass of her people without detracting greatly from their sense of freedom, Asia will be lost to Communism. If India, on the other hand, demonstrates that democratic government can ensure not only economic security but individual liberty, then Asia will be won to democracy. What India and China are today in fact doing is wrestling for the political soul of Asia. That is why India's role in Asian affairs is crucial and vital.

The difference between the two is that Communism is a crusading creed eager to propagate its doctrines abroad, but democracy is too often content to let the facts speak for themselves. Aggression is implicit in the Communism of Stalin and Mao, for Marxism as they understand it can fulfil itself only by spreading the gospel far and wide. This is the new imperialism. The old imperialism, eager for economic exploitation, sought dominion over the bodies of men, striving through them to reach its objectives of cheap raw materials and cheap labour. The new imperialism would imprison and overawe men's minds.

In Communist China's eyes Japan, not India, constitutes the major threat to her position in the Far East. America, having inherited Japanese responsibilities in the Pacific, is inevitably identified with this hostility, which Washington's support to Chiang Kai-shek, its defence of South Korea and aid to France in Indo-China accentuate to fever heat. For all practical purposes Peking regards Japan as an American colony, a view shared largely by the rest of Asia. The identification of the old enemy, Japan, with the new enemy, America, gives pith and point to Chinese fears and hate.

On the other hand, India, in Asian eyes, is both free and democratic. Both India and neighbouring Burma have reacted strongly to the Communists inside their borders; and Indian leaders, though inclined to deprecate the possibilities of military penetration across the rugged terrain of the Himalayas, are wide awake to the possibilities of an infiltration of ideologies from across the frontier.

This is to present the problem starkly. What many educated Indians find difficult to understand is America's allergy to their country's foreign policy. Since independence the pattern of Indian history has followed closely the pattern of American history in the early decades after 1787. Like America, India started internally with the consolidation of the States. Externally she seeks to avoid foreign entanglements much as America did in the long years ending with the two world wars.

The foundations of United States foreign policy in this period were twofold: Freedom of the Seas, or the Open Door; and Peace by Arbitration. "Neutrality" was a term of which Americans were not ashamed. From Washington's Farewell Address of September 17, 1796, it would seem as if the fierce antagonisms engendered by the French Revolution touched the New World not at all. "Europe," declared Washington, "has a set of primary interests which to us have none, or a very remote relation. . . . It must be unwise in us to implicate ourselves, by artificial ties, in the ordinary vicissitudes of her politics or the ordinary combinations and collisions of her friendships or enmities."

Over a hundred years later Woodrow Wilson, in a message to his countrymen in the first year of the First World War, adjured them to "be neutral not only in deed but in words and thoughts." Three years passed before America took the plunge. In the twilight between the two wars isolationism gathered strength. Hitler reverberated across the Atlantic; but only in December, 1941, after Japan had attacked Pearl Harbor, did the United States enter the war against the dictators.

To many in India it seems odd that a country which was neu-

tral for three of the four years of World War I and for two of
the five years of World War II should resent neutrality in another
country—and that in peace, not war. A country's foreign policy
is motivated by enlightened self-interest. This consideration
frankly governs India's policy. But to infer from it that Nehru
is no democrat, and that India seeks affiliations outside the democratic camp, would be as malicious and absurd as to suggest that
America's real sympathies in the opening years of World Wars I
and II lay respectively with the Kaiser and Hitler.

Admittedly the times have changed. Science, by annihilating
distances, has made nonsense of old logic and logistics. The intrusion of atomic power should revolutionise geopolitical thinking,
for in the atom age a base at Helsinki no more safeguards the
heart of Moscow than Okinawa or the Philippines protects San
Francisco. Certain fundamental truths survive despite the march
of science. One of them is that power blocs are an incitement to
war, not an insurance against it. The more eagerly nations seek
security through alliances, the more rapidly they drift to inse-
curity. At some stage an immovable object must clash with an
irresistible force.

A fact insufficiently appreciated in the Western world is that
throughout Asia, and particularly in India, the emphasis is more
on the community than on the individual. Hinduism comprises a
complex of innumerable social groups, "a mighty forest with a
thousand waving arms." Though Hinduism is a matter of personal faith, Hindu society operates on a community or clan
basis. Its two props are caste and the joint family. If the Hindu
community is broken down into units the basic digit is not the
individual but the joint family, an institution blending the Roman
principle of *pater familias* with the primitive concept of com-
munal welfare. In Hindu society the individual is subordinate to
the group.

Thus Russia and China with their emphasis on the welfare of
the community and the State exercise a stronger gravitational
pull than America, home of private enterprise and the freedom

of the individual. In many Eastern eyes, America mistakes the means for the end. By exalting private enterprise and the individual, she makes the acquisition of wealth for wealth's sake an end in itself. This, of course, is not true. But it is thus that the American scene presents itself to the general Asian gaze.

Russia, on the other hand, appears to subordinate the interests of the individual to the larger interests of the group; and, in a society motivated by a similar urge, the fact registers. This does not mean that Hinduism approximates to Communism. As against the colourless uniformity of the Marxist, the Hindu strives to reach out to a rich harmony of life and living. It has been well said that the Hindu solution seeks unity of religion not in a common creed but in a common quest. The goal is not unity of organisation but unity of spirit.

Although Moscow has denounced Nehru more than once as "a running dog of Western Imperialism," its pressure tactics on the highly sensitive governments and peoples of renascent Asia are often more subtle than those of Washington. Communism operates behind a mask. It has its fifth column in every country. Thus its pressures appear to be indigenous when in fact they are external. The reactions of the Western world are more direct and therefore more resented. Russia's hand is rarely evident, but her voice is omnivocal.

Russia has another ace in the colour question. Whatever be the inhibitions of the Soviet State, colour has no place in its social calculus; and that fact profoundly impresses Asia. It is true that the Jews were the targets of Moscow's venomous attacks during the Czech trials of 1952; and, though this was noted in India, it created less stir than a Negro lynching would in the United States. Americans, sensitive to reproach on the Negro problem, sometimes counter by pointing to the practice of untouchability in India. As against their own active antipathies Hinduism, they allege, is capable of much passive cruelty. The charge is valid and legitimate. But aside from the fact that two wrongs do not make a right, the Indian Constitution makes untouchability a statutory offence by expressly abolishing it in its Chapter of Fundamental Rights and forbidding its practice in any form. On the other hand, the fact that discriminatory practices against the Negro have the sanction of law in certain American States is noted by Asia.

India has no illusions about Communism, though some of her leaders unfortunately cherish romantic notions on the country's relationship with China. They like to idealise Mao as a benevolent Buddha eager for Asian peace and friendship. So he is—but on his own terms. Here India's danger lies in being an unconscious accessory to Communist China, in aiding and abetting her plans until the Chinese Frankenstein swallows up Asia, including India. To recognise the character and ambitions of your neighbour does not necessarily imply that you must shake your fist at him. What puzzles Asia is that the shambles of two world wars has taught the world nothing. War, as Nehru recognises, is a lunatic solution which solves nothing. Even in our atomic age China faced by an invading force might possibly still be able to trade space for time. In a long war of attrition she can draw more easily on her man power; and psychologically she is more prepared than any Western power for blood, tears, toil, and sweat. A war fought on Chinese soil might well be inconclusive, leaving the Communist government more entrenched in the hearts of a suffering people than it now is. A war will solve nothing.

The question our generation has to face is whether a war between Communism and democracy is inevitable. Can the two systems subsist side by side at peace with each other, or must they inevitably collide? It is an odd fact that men generally think through their stomachs rather than through their minds. When hunger and scarcity affect millions of men they begin to ask questions. From the economic point of view the folly of dividing the world into two camps is self-evident. Behind the iron curtain are rich resources of grain and foodstuffs which Western Europe, Asia, and the world would welcome. Behind the iron curtain again are countries in need of capital machinery and goods which the

United States and part of Western Europe could supply. Sino-Japanese trade was long complementary. Japan's hunger for the raw materials of Manchuria led to expansionism and war.

America seeks to underwrite the democratic world. But how long can she afford to go on doing this? Marshall Aid in Europe halted the Soviet Moloch in his tracks. But simultaneously it diverted him from the Occident to the Orient. Before Asia can use guns she must have bread. If American aid and dollars could ensure political stability in Greece, Italy, and France, why should the trickle of Point Four be thinned by hesitations and doubts about the political stability of Asia's newborn independent countries? Political freedom has salvaged these lands for democracy from Communism. If India, Pakistan, Burma, and Indonesia are in the democratic camp today it is because they gained their independence in good time. The Burmese government is even today engaged in a war with its Communists. And the Indian government's reaction to the indigenous Reds is notoriously drastic. Had France relinquished her hold on Indo-China, Ho Chi Minh might today have been the leader of a democratic Viet Nam. A loosening of foreign political bonds in Asia must accompany an accretion of economic aid.

Whether Asia goes Communist now depends less on the West than on the two major nations of that continent, China and India. India today constitutes the main bastion of democracy in Asia. Japan, operating in what is interpreted as an imperialistic shadow of which Asia is acutely conscious, is an uncertain factor in Asian calculations of democracy and freedom. Japan may be democratic—but is she free? So Asia asks. But India is free—and democratic.